Thinking About Faith in God

How Belief Makes Science Possible

Jonathan Clatworthy

Fortress Press

Minneapolis

THINKING ABOUT FAITH IN GOD
How Belief Makes Science Possible

Fortress Press Edition © 2015
Copyright © Jonathan Clatworthy 2012

This book is published in cooperation with Society for Promoting Christian Knowledge, London, England. Originally titled *Making Sense of Faith in God: How Belief Makes Science Possible*. Interior contents have not been changed.

Unless otherwise noted, Scripture quotations are taken from the New Revised Standard Version of the Bible, Anglicized Edition, copyright © 1989, 1995 by the Division of Christian Education of the National Council of the Churches of Christ in the USA. Used by permission. All rights reserved.

Library of Congress Cataloging-in-Publication Data
Print ISBN: 978-1-5064-0067-9
eBook ISBN: 978-1-5064-0097-6

The paper used in this publication meets the minimum requirements of American National Standard for Information Services—Permanence of Paper for Printed Library Materials, ANSIZ329.48-1984.

Manufactured in the U.S.A.

Thinking About
Faith in God

Contents

Preface

The Modern Church 'Making Sense of Christianity' series aims to defend Christianity by offering accounts of it that make sense to the modern mind. Many people are put off Christianity because the versions they have heard of seem superstitious, anti-scientific or immoral. We hope these books will help make Christianity accessible to those seeking a credible account of how we relate to the divine, inviting readers to affirm rather than suspend their critical faculties. Each book focuses on one contentious issue.

To some, perhaps, these books may seem destructive, as they challenge certain versions of Christianity. The intention, however, is constructive. Christianity as it is sometimes expressed demands a stance of defiance, refusing to accept modern society's beliefs about evolution, or gender equality, or whatever symbol of difference is current at the time. These books respond to society more positively, with critical support. By and large we welcome modern society's search for understanding and its new insights. The support remains critical because what seems true at any one time may later turn out to be mistaken, and we expect Christianity to be a constructive contributor to modern knowledge, offering insights as well as receiving them.

The focus of this book is God. Although the idea is declining, many still believe that science has disproved God's existence. I aim to show that the claims of science are supported, rather than denied, by the belief that there is a divine being, a creative mind with intentions and values.

The text is an edited version of a series of lectures I gave at St Bride's Church, Liverpool, in 2010 and 2011. The discussions on those occasions enabled me to clarify the issues, and I am especially grateful for the contributions of Steve Flatt and Petra Elsmore. I have been greatly helped by discussions with supportive friends who are unbelievers; as well as Steve, discussions with Paul Doran, John Halliday and others at the local branch of Philosophy in Pubs have helped me think through the issues. I am also grateful to Paul Badham and my wife Marguerite for reading the text, spotting errors and advising improvements in a supportive manner.

I have tried to avoid repeating ground covered in my earlier books, but Chapter 1 summarizes a case made at greater length in *Liberal Faith in a Divided Church* (O Books, 2008) and Chapter 4 makes a similar case to Chapter 7 of *Good God: Green Theology and the Value of Creation* (Jon Carpenter, 1997).

I have finished writing this book at a time when world capitalism is in crisis. The Occupy movement is growing. EU leaders are agonizing over Greece's debts and which country will be next. It may seem that analysing theories about God is an unnecessary luxury. I believe the opposite. If human minds are the only minds capable of working out what we ought to do, then the best humanity will ever do is serve the interests of the most powerful. If, on the other hand, a wiser, more benign mind is responsible for the way we have evolved, then it makes sense to hope that humanity can rise above self-interest and achieve a better way of living.

Introduction

Modern society does not know what to do with God. For many, God belongs in a small box labelled 'religion', and is not expected to appear outside it. Maybe the box itself is a useless bequest from the past, fit only to be thrown out. Or maybe it is one of many optional lifestyle choices: like *Star Trek* or horse racing, people may engage with it without feeling any need to justify it.

Traditional religions have understood God very differently. Making sense of God has been an essential starting point for making sense of anything at all. This book will explain why.

I found myself challenged by the difference between these perspectives in the 1980s. I was helping to organize the annual Green Fair in Sheffield. Hundreds of people came, many feeling a need for a spiritual dimension to their lives and hoping to shop around for guidance. They were interested in a wide range of traditions, from crystal therapy to Indian meditation methods to Tai Chi to dancing naked round some standing stones in the Peak District under a full moon. I was struck by the wide variety of providers. Nevertheless the number of providers was less than the number of Christian churches in the city, and none of those people told me they had tried going to a Christian church. It was as though that was something they definitely did not want.

Being a Christian priest I wanted to know why. I learned to appreciate that people who deliberately engage on a spiritual search usually expect to remain in control of their own searching process, so the last thing they want is someone who claims to know all the answers, burdens them with a mountain of beliefs and makes them feel guilty for any doubts they may have. If this is what many expected from Christian churches, I felt I understood. I knew of churches which promoted evangelism as an unequal dialogue where

> People who deliberately engage on a spiritual search usually expect to remain in control of their own searching process

the Christian knows the truth and does all the talking. Spiritual seekers, on enquiring about Christianity, might find that their own views were not taken seriously. I also knew of churches which taught that reason cannot convert, so becoming a Christian is primarily a matter of having a personal conversion experience. Non-Christians being evangelized might then feel they were being subjected to emotional manipulation rather than being credited with the ability to make their own judgements. It is hardly surprising when people with a spiritual awareness do not want to buy into packages of dogma which they do not find convincing. They often avoid speaking of having a 'belief' at all because of the dogmatic connotations of the word; they may prefer to speak more vaguely of having a 'spirituality'.

I was left with three questions, all of which are even more relevant today than they were then. First, why are so many people prepared to spend time and effort trying to establish a spiritual dimension to their lives? What are they missing, that makes them feel they need it? Second, if a spiritual dimension is so important, why are so many people starting from scratch with an open mind? Why have they been brought up without such a dimension – or at least, without one they find acceptable? Third, why do so many people fail to find the spiritual guidance they seek in Christian churches?

This book will address these questions. They are closely related to each other, but the emphasis will be on the first. What seems to have become the default position in modern western culture is that there is no God. Recently this position has been defended by a number of 'new atheist' authors, the best known of whom are Richard Dawkins, the late Christopher Hitchens and Daniel Dennett.[1] Their main argument is that science can explain the way the universe works without any need for God. Either God's existence has been completely disproved, or at least there is no evidence for it; so believing is either a pointless optional extra or, worse, a misleading superstition.

These authors then proceed to describe other versions of Christianity and Islam as merely watered-down versions of those dogmatic fundamentalisms

Their main target is the God of fundamentalist and dogmatic religion in the forms which have been flourishing over the last generation or two, especially in the USA. Such versions of Christianity and Islam often do reject scientific findings; opposition to evolution, for example, is common. These authors then proceed to describe other versions of Christianity and Islam as merely watered-down versions of those dogmatic fundamentalisms. In this way they make their task easier, as it gives them an excuse to ignore better informed accounts of religious belief.

On the one hand their books have been so popular that they clearly touch a raw nerve: many people have indeed had strong negative experiences of religious teaching of this type, and are anxious to have nothing to do with it. On the other hand, many people are dissatisfied with the conviction that there is no God. They feel a need to relate to *something*: something which they can integrate into the rest of their life and help them make sense of it, without buying into dogmas which defy ordinary modern knowledge of the world. Faced with a choice between rejecting all spiritual awareness and rejecting modern scientific knowledge, it is understandable if many prefer to keep their options open. The result is a range of vaguely 'spiritual' practices and ideas which can be picked up and dropped with minimal commitment, in a culture reluctant to subject any of them to rigorous examination. This book, as the title indicates, offers a different alternative: to reject neither reason nor God, because believing in God makes sense.

Nineteenth-century atheism and dogmatism

Thus modern western society is slowly moving into a new phase. For nearly two centuries, from the end of the eighteenth century until the 1960s, many educated people believed science was about to disprove, or had already disproved, the existence of God. It seemed that religious belief was a relic from a superstitious past, destined to die out as we all became better educated. Christians often reacted by appealing to spiritual truths beyond the reach of science, thereby creating more fundamentalist and dogmatic versions of Christianity.

The result was a debate between two positions that had a great deal in common with each other. Atheists denounced all religion as irrational, and so denied the existence of God in the name of reason. Religious

From then on, militant atheism and religious dogmatism have fed on each other

3

dogmatists agreed that reason and God were incompatible, but rejected secular reason in the name of God. From then on, militant atheism and religious dogmatism have fed on each other, denouncing each other while dismissing more liberal religious traditions as watered-down, inauthentic versions.

Since the 1970s the tide has turned. Increasing numbers have been convinced that there is more to reality than science can show us. They may prefer to speak of having a spirituality rather than a religion, but they feel a desire to engage with a deeper reality, whatever-it-is that underpins the everyday things of our ordinary lives.

This perhaps explains why the 'new atheist' authors express such intense bitterness against religious belief. Their arguments, far from riding the crest of a wave, are better seen as reactionary defences of an outdated tradition, by people lamenting the failure of an older hope that religious belief would die out.

At the same time, what people experience in the Christian churches often seems equally reactionary and outdated. Instead of encouraging spiritual searchers and offering Christian resources for people to use as they see fit, churches often continue using the anti-rational methods they learned against atheism, proudly advertising those elements of their tradition which are hardest to justify rationally. This clash of ideologies, with both sides determined to deny that believing in God makes sense, increasingly feels like a voice from the past.

When it comes to believing in God, therefore, the two most loudly trumpeted options are incompatible with each other: either God, or modern science and reason. This either/or dichotomy results from a most unusual history, not at all the way most societies, or most people in the past, have thought about the matter.

Chapter 1 will describe how we got into our present situation. One of the advantages of a good awareness of history is that it helps us appreciate how ideas change. What seems obviously true today did not always seem obviously true, and sometimes may have seemed obviously false. This is certainly the case with believing in God: given that where we are now is a most unusual place to be, how on earth did we get here? The story cannot be told without acknowledging the close interaction between anti-religious theories and anti-rational religious dogmatism.

The rest of the book is more positively concerned with exploring the reasons why people do believe in God, and how well they can be justified. Chapters 2, 3, 4 and 5 focus on the most common reasons for belief: design, values, morality and experience. These chapters generate some theoretical questions, which will be the topic of the following three chapters. By the end it should be clear that a pattern is emerging: to reject God consistently we would need to redescribe reality in the bleakest, simplest terms, and this would mean denying most of our ordinary experience. The coherent alternative is that reality as we experience it makes better sense if there is more to it than we experience.

This book does not defend one account of God against others. It draws on Christian resources because these are the ones I am familiar with, but it is not about Christianity as such. Nor does it defend the idea of a *good* God against the common argument that such a being would not have allowed all the suffering and evil in the world. Important though this question is, the focus here is on making sense of the reasons why people *do* believe in God. We shall therefore be concerned with how to *justify* belief. Psychological and sociological motivations are another matter; they may produce strong desires to believe, regardless of whether God exists.

Before proceeding with this more positive agenda, however, I need to justify some of the claims I have already made about the oddness of the present situation. If we can understand why Europeans broke with earlier tradition to produce God-free accounts of reality, it may help us appreciate which bits of our inheritance are worth keeping and which are no longer of value.

1

Our very strange situation

————•—•—•————

Belief in some kind of divine being is normal. Throughout human history nearly all societies have claimed to relate to one or more gods. Only modern Europe, from the seventeenth century onwards, has produced societies that treat belief in the divine as a dispensable option, and only in the last century have other parts of the world imported the idea.

Atheism appeals to science. Characteristically, it claims that scientific facts describe the real nature of the world, and are therefore the key to progress, while values and religious beliefs are mere human inventions – at best unnecessary options but perhaps harmful superstitions.

This story jars with most people. Successive governments try to persuade more students to study science, but students persist in wanting to study the humanities. Far more people read novels than science books, and far more television viewers watch soap operas than documentaries on new technology. In public we may go along with the secular picture, but most of us live as though we do not want to live in a world like that. Why?

The scientific facts, the 'how' questions, are important for some people at some times, but the 'why' questions are important to all of us. Scientists believe the universe began with a Big Bang. Most of us do not need to know how it began; but most of us, at some stage in our lives, will be in a state of utter despair and will ask questions like 'Why does it have to be like this?'

Other societies take the 'why' questions seriously, and integrate them with the 'how' questions. The normal way to explore them is through stories. Many of these stories have been dismissed by modern westerners as 'myths', as though they were just bad science, but this is to misunderstand them. Like our novels and soap operas, they help people explore what happens in life, how to evaluate it, and how to respond. In response to some things it is appropriate to have a good cry, in response to others it is appropriate to be astonished. Some things are to be resisted, others accepted. We learn appropriate responses through stories.

One example is bereavement. Suppose the person you love most of all dies. The doctor comes, you burst into tears, and you say 'Why?' It would be a crass doctor indeed who said, 'I can tell you why. The heart stopped beating and the lungs stopped breathing.' That would not help at all.

Rather more helpful would be an ancient Hittite myth about a goddess who was preparing for battle and asked a human man for help. (Part of the story has been lost, so I am depending on a reconstruction.) The man consented, on condition that he could spend the night with her. She agreed. He ended up moving in with her. However, she laid down one rule: he was never under any circumstances to look out of the window. One day temptation got the better of him, he looked out of the window, and there he saw his wife and children. He begged for permission to return to them. He went back to his family and thereby lost the chance of immortality.[1]

This story, much like a good novel or play, faces the listener with an inescapable question: 'Which would I have chosen? Would I rather live in a land where people live for ever and nobody is ever young, or would I rather live for a limited time, in a land with babies, children and families, and let them succeed me when I am old and nothing is new or exciting for me any more?' By reflecting on these questions we are helped to appreciate that there is indeed a proper time for death. Although we are upset to lose our loved ones, life without death would not be better.

All over the world there are traditional stories like this, reflecting on the big questions. Where do I come from? Where does my family, or village, come from? Why do people die? Are animals the same as us, or different? Why is childbirth so painful? Why do we find some things funny? Why do we get so much pleasure from sex? Why do people kill each other? Characteristically they combine what we would now call the scientific answers, the 'how', with the value answers, the 'why'. If we treat them purely as science of course we now have more accurate answers, but they were more than this.

We should not imagine that everybody believed every detail of those stories; after all, good stories survive outside their original settings. They do however show how, in order to reflect on the 'why' questions, we need to assume the existence of real values transcending our own minds. The reason why these traditional stories usually refer to one or more divine beings is that if we are to justify our feelings and values we need to ground them in something bigger than ourselves. Feelings and values only exist where there are minds capable of feeling and evaluating. We shall explore this further in Chapter 3.

In order to reflect on the 'why' questions, we need to assume the existence of real values transcending our own minds

Medieval debates

Why did Europeans end up excluding the divine from their explanations of ordinary life? I shall begin the story in the Middle Ages, because this is the time when European society first debated the relationship between reason and God as an issue in its own right. Before then, in the ancient Roman Empire some Christians had denounced mere human reason in the interests of divine revelation, but without producing theories about reason itself; they had merely done what people do when they are losing an argument. Otherwise, throughout the ancient era Christians used every rational tool at their disposal in intense, centuries-long debates about theological issues like the Trinity and how Jesus could be both God and human. From the sixth century to the tenth, educational standards in western Europe were low; and because it was the monasteries which preserved ancient knowledge, church leaders came to be the leading authorities on learning in general. They normally allowed new ideas unless they contradicted what had been inherited from the ancients, especially the Bible. This became the conservative position against which scholars reacted when educational standards began to rise again.

With the revival, new questions arose. Genesis 1.7 says God put water above the sky. In the twelfth century William of Conches denied

Some, however, were so committed to defending the Bible that they refused to accept any new idea that contradicted a biblical text

that there was any such water, and thereby inflamed debate about the Bible's authority. A power struggle developed in the places of learning. Theologians continued to work within the integrated view of reality, expecting traditional beliefs about God and the Bible to contribute to developing theories about the world. Some, however, were so committed to defending the Bible that they refused to accept any new idea that contradicted a biblical text. Recently atheist campaigners have often exaggerated this opposition and accused the Church of opposing science. In fact the question at issue was how to balance the different authorities against each other when they disagreed, in an age which had not yet established the principle of seeking answers by conducting experiments. In retrospect we can now say that sometimes the new ideas were right and the biblical texts were wrong, but sometimes it was the other way round; for example, many researchers accepted Aristotle's view that the world had existed from eternity, while the Church taught that it had come into existence at a point in time.

Another issue was the use of logic in theology. Medieval education emphasized logic so much that early scholastics hoped it could prove the truth of Christian doctrines. In the eleventh century Anselm thought he could logically prove that God exists, that God is a Trinity, and that God had to become a human. Later scholastics were more sceptical and increasingly concluded that these doctrines must have been directly revealed to the Church by God.[2] In fact they had been hammered out in centuries of debate in the early Church; but the later medievals treated them as direct divine revelation.

These issues led to a dualistic theory of knowledge. According to the theory there are two ways of knowing things: physical matter is observable and can be studied by reason, while spiritual things are not observable so the only way we can know about them is by direct revelation from God through the Bible and the Church's teaching. This separation meant late medieval theologians could study spiritual matters while natural philosophers – the forerunners of modern scientists – could study physical matters, without either side encroaching on the other.

This dualism permitted researchers to develop theories about the world even when they contradicted a biblical text. Far from denying God, they were merely appealing to God's gift of reason as opposed to that other gift, revelation. While the study of the physical world was thus freed from church censorship it was also limited, especially by the principle of observability. Whatever could not be observed was counted as spiritual, not physical, and therefore was in the domain of the Church's teaching. Most medievals believed the world was full of invisible angels and demons, self-willed beings going about their business in ways that affected humans and therefore made the physical world unpredictable. This would have made science impossible; at that stage it was essential to reject anything that could not be observed. Scientists today, however, believe in many unobservables, from subatomic particles to dark matter.[3]

While late medieval dualism had unforeseen effects on science, the idea that all spiritual knowledge is contained within divine revelation had a disastrous effect on religious belief. First, it meant that any new spiritual idea is by definition wrong because everything we can possibly know is already in the Bible. This gave western Christianity that backward-looking character which it often has today, for example in debates about women and gays. Second, because all spiritual truth was to be found in the Bible there was no point in dialogue with other faiths. They were all just plain wrong. Again, this idea remains popular in many Christian circles today. Third, it meant that knowledge of spiritual matters, being a direct product of divine revelation, was absolutely certain to be true. Whenever a biblical teaching seemed impossible, immoral or contradictory, it revealed the limits not of the Bible but of human reason. Nobody had any business doubting or questioning any item of revelation. This idea is echoed today by those Christians who are quick to denounce 'human reason'. Finally, it gave immense power to church leaders. They became the gatekeepers of all spiritual knowledge. Today this feature is most obvious in the case of Roman Catholicism, but it remains common among Protestants too.

Thus late medieval dualism changed the nature of western Christianity. Instead of the rich proliferation of ideas that had characterized its earlier phases, it came to seem that Christians ought to agree with each other on all spiritual matters. Such an idea seemed possible when the papacy could be accepted as the unchallenged authority on biblical interpretation. Soon the Reformation blew it open. Protestants and Catholics disagreed about what divine revelation is and who its gate-keepers are. To make matters worse, both sides believed that revelation is to be accepted without question, as superior to all human reason, and this left them without any way to resolve their disagreements. The theoretical crisis generated two centuries of religious wars, and still produces sectarian disputes today.

Enlightenment reason

Eventually reason had to make a comeback. The Enlightenment, often called the Age of Reason, was mainly provoked by the religious wars. Enlightenment accounts of reason are broadly of two types, a wider one and a narrower one. According to the wider account the human mind has many different processes. This was the view held by Thomas Aquinas in the Middle Ages and in the Enlightenment by the Cambridge Platonists and Joseph Butler. Today philosophers and psychologists continue to analyse how we come to know things; a typical list would include the evidence of our senses, rational deduction, instinct, intuition and memory. These processes do not produce absolute certainty: we think we know things, but we may be wrong.

For some this was inadequate. The early Enlightenment philosophers wanted to show how reason could bring the religious wars to an end. They could see that people kept fighting because each side claimed absolute certainty for its own views. Enlightenment philosophers there-fore presented reason as a better way to establish certainty. To do this they limited reason to logic and the evidence of the senses.

René Descartes proposed to base all knowledge on a self-evident starting point, his 'I think, therefore I am'. From this certainty he pro-ceeded to deduce, as also certain, the existence of God and the physical world. Philosophers describe his system as 'rationalism': here reason is about analytical thinking, deducing.[4]

Whereas medieval dualism had been about two ways of knowing things, Descartes turned it into two distinct realms of reality, one physical and the other spiritual. The physical one is observable and deterministic, nothing but atoms pushing each other according to laws of nature. The spiritual one is where the human soul relates to God. This separation of the spiritual from the material set God at a distance from the world and presented the human being as basically a soul which happens to have a body.

The other main element in the narrow account of reason is information from the senses, 'empiricism'. John Locke believed the human mind has only three faculties: it is aware of its own inner states and operations, it receives information through the five senses and it can make logical deductions. Nothing else. These, he believed, are the processes on which all knowledge is built.[5] More ambitious than the medieval dualists, he set out to show that even his narrow reason, limited to the evidence of the senses and logical deduction, could still establish the truth of the Christian faith.

Central to his argument was the evidence from miracles. Today miracles are usually understood as events which break the laws of nature. Science works by gathering data and generalizing from it to establish regularities. If the study of physical processes had not discovered regularities we would not be able to explain how things work or make predictions. Science, therefore, is only possible because we can explain the processes of nature in terms of regularities. We call these regularities the laws of nature.

Most religions today affirm and value this ability to establish laws of nature; we shall explore the reasons later. Before the rise of modern science Jews, Christians and Muslims believed that God is in control of the way the world works, so a term like 'laws of nature' could only mean that God does most things regularly and a 'miracle', as its derivation from the Latin *miraculum* implies, was something to be wondered at – usually because it meant God had done something irregularly. As Augustine wrote,

> We say, as a matter of course, that all portents are contrary to nature. But they are not. For how can an event be contrary to nature when it happens by the will of God, since the will of the great Creator assuredly is the nature of every created thing? A portent, therefore, does not occur contrary to nature, but contrary to what is known of nature.[6]

Because of the tensions between the claims of 'faith' and 'reason', as described above, early modern scientists tended to treat the laws of nature as real powers. As a result they came to understand miracles differently, as events that break the laws of nature. Locke used this idea in his argument for the truth of Christianity. His argument ran: the Bible records miracles, only God can perform miracles, so the events described in the Bible must have been performed by God. God, he believed, performed them in order to reveal that Christianity is the true religion.[7]

It is a bad argument. We can be confident that a brilliant mind like Locke's would not have used it if a better one had been available. Fifty years later David Hume turned it on its head: the Bible records miracles, miracles cannot happen because they break the laws of nature, so the Bible contains falsehoods. Miracles, he says,

> are observed chiefly to abound among ignorant and barbarous nations; or if a civilized people has ever given admission to any of them, that people will be found to have received them from ignorant and barbarous ancestors ... When we peruse the first histories of all nations, we are apt to imagine ourselves transported into some new world; where the whole frame of nature is disjointed, and every element performs its operations in a different manner, from what it does at present ... *It is strange*, a judicious reader is apt to say, upon the perusal of these wonderful historians, *that such prodigious events never happen in our days.*[8]

What Locke and Hume had in common was the conviction that the laws of nature are real powers, normally unbreakable. They disagreed about whether God had the power to break them. Their disagreement remains part of religious debate today; conservative Christians often imagine that Christians have always believed what Locke believed, while their atheist counterparts imagine that Hume has refuted religious belief in general. In fact the authors of the Bible and earlier Christians did not share Locke's understanding of miracles. Nor do philosophers of science today.

The laws of nature are observed regularities, not forces

Although scientists have established many laws of nature, in each case what has been established is a regular process of the type 'when x happens, y happens'; in other words the laws of nature are observed regularities, not forces. What makes them happen is another matter, to which we shall return in Chapter 7.

Similar to Locke's argument from miracles is interventionism, often called the 'God of the gaps' argument. This idea, favoured by Isaac Newton, points to the processes in the universe which science cannot explain, and deduces that they can only be explained by divine intervention. Like the argument from miracles it appeals to the belief that only God can break the laws of nature. It is now largely discredited because it has so often appealed to processes which science could not explain, only to find that science later explained them.

Modern ideas about religion owe a great deal to Locke and Hume. Locke, responding to the wars of religion, argued that churches should be voluntary societies without the right to dictate how the state should be governed; it should be reason, not religion, that determined government policies. Thus he paved the way for seeing religion as something one voluntarily opts into. Hume, accepting this view, asked many questions about why anyone would want to opt into it – especially if reason, not religion, provided the tools for understanding reality. Although there is some continuing debate about whether Hume believed in God, he was the first penetrating thinker to think about religion from the perspective of a non-believing outsider.

With the benefit of hindsight we can see that the early Enlightenment philosophers were trying to do the impossible. They were right to reaffirm reason, wrong to think that logic and the evidence of the senses could produce complete and certain knowledge.

When this became clear there were two possible responses. One was to return to a wider account of reason and abandon the search for certainty. This is the main way philosophers describe knowledge today. The other was to carry on insisting that narrow reason can provide a complete and certain account of reality, and reinterpret all human experience accordingly.

Hobbes' *Leviathan*, published in 1650, popularized the idea that everything that exists is reducible to atoms pushing each other in accordance with laws of nature. The tradition called 'materialism' developed, arguing that the universe is like Descartes' physical realm but is all there is. 'Positivism' adds to this the claim that narrow reason – just logic, mathematics and the evidence of the senses – is able to establish complete and certain knowledge of it.

Positivists made ambitious claims for science. Today their most characteristic claims are that science produces facts while religion can only produce beliefs and opinions, and that science has disproved the existence of God.

Positivism was at its most popular in the nineteenth century. By the end of the century, however, it was undermining itself. If all knowledge is based on human experience, and if everything is observable, then we should dispense with God; but we should also dispense with all metaphysical ideas, some of which are essential to science. If you hold this book in your hand and then move your fingers apart, the book will fall downwards. We assume that the movement of the fingers, together with gravity, causes the book to drop. However we never see causes. We only ever infer them. Because they cannot be observed, according to the positivist principle they do not exist. By the end of the nineteenth century positivism had lost its earlier optimism. Confidence that narrow reason would explain everything had turned into a conviction that nothing existed except what narrow reason could explain. Ernst Mach, for example, argued that the physical objects we see are just bundles of sensory experiences to which we give names. If you look at something which you think is a wooden table, all you actually see is a brown shape. To infer that it is a table is, he argued, to go beyond what we can know.[9]

Positivism was popular for a time because it seemed to explain how science produces real knowledge with certainty. It is now accepted that science does not produce certainties. Instead it asks questions, gathers data and develops hypotheses. Some hypotheses are more likely to be true than others, but in principle they are all open to review when new evidence calls them into question. It is this refusal to close down further research which has made science so fruitful. One of its most significant findings is that reality is far more complex than the human mind can even conceive. There is no way we shall ever know everything, let alone with certainty. Today positivism has been largely rejected, but it remains the main argument driving militant atheism.

It is not, however, the only source. Today many people are brought up in families where God is not discussed, so unbelief can be an inherited assumption. In the past to disbelieve was to make a deliberate stand. Why did increasing numbers of people make it?

16

As far as we know there were very few atheists before the seventeenth century. It was not until the eighteenth that significant numbers denied the existence of God, with the educated classes in France taking the lead. In the nineteenth, church leaders saw atheism as their greatest threat. The main arguments for it were materialism and positivism, which seems to suggest that it developed as a theoretical philosophy.

However, there was also a practical motive. Even in the early seventeenth century Puritans were writing tracts warning people against losing their faith, thereby giving Satan another soul to torment in hell for eternity. There were so many of these tracts that there must have been many Puritans losing their faith. We do not have writings by people who lost their faith at that time, but judging from the tracts it is easy enough to see what was happening. Puritan teaching had it that all humans are wicked sinners and deserve to spend eternity suffering agony in hell, but God chooses to elect a small minority to a blessed afterlife in heaven. People worried about their own destiny. A common doctrine was that if you live a godfearing life and are blessed with the outward signs of success – like money – they may be God's sign that you are one of the elect who will go to heaven. For those who did live an upright life and had plenty of money, this would have been a comforting thing to believe. It does not take much imagination, however, to appreciate how it would strike the ears of a pregnant unmarried girl or a man who could not earn enough to keep his family. It would seem that an eternity in hell was in store. We know many people spent their lives in terror at what was to come after death; it would hardly be surprising if some preferred to believe there is no God at all.[10]

This is no more than a likely reconstruction; for the seventeenth century the evidence is insufficient. For the nineteenth century we are on firmer ground. When historians ask why so many educated people lost their faith then, the evidence indicates that it was rarely for scientific or philosophical reasons: usually it was for moral reasons, the most common being that they could not believe in hell.

Thus we have two accounts of the rise of atheism, a theoretical one about how the world works and a practical response to personal anxiety. Atheists naturally prefer the theoretical account because they think it is true; church leaders usually also prefer it because they do not want to believe that their doctrines have driven people to atheism. As a result modern debates about the existence of God often focus on theoretical arguments which may be irrelevant to the real reasons for disbelief.

> Church leaders usually also prefer it because they do not want to believe that their doctrines have driven people to atheism

Over time atheism became so common that belief in God could no longer be taken for granted as normal. All societies need an overall worldview, or 'paradigm', to hold together their various accounts of reality within a unified account of what the world is like, what human beings are like, and how therefore we should live. In the Middle Ages the Catholic Church provided the paradigm. Theology was the Queen of the Sciences, holding together law, politics, science, theology, ethics, medicine and mathematics in an overall account of reality. Many dissented from what the Church taught; but dissent was turned into crisis by the Reformation, when there was no longer agreement about what the true Church was.

In the medieval paradigm Christianity held the ring, setting the parameters within which different accounts of reason, knowledge and government could be debated. In the Enlightenment paradigm reason held the ring, within which different accounts of religion could be debated just like other issues. Since then each institution and each subject of research has taken trouble to establish its independence from religious authority, sometimes in the teeth of church leaders desperately trying to hang on to whatever authority they still had.

Eventually the secular paradigm established a new role for religion. All religious beliefs were only to apply within a distinct, self-contained sphere of religion, and had no relevance to anything outside. As a result religious belief became an optional extra, unnecessary for understanding reality. Religion had been put in its box.

> Religious belief became an optional extra, unnecessary for understanding reality

This means that just as we do not mention cosines except when discussing geometry, so also we should not mention God except when specifically talking about religion. The matter of God remains a sensitive issue, a taboo. Those brought up to take the taboo for granted may not realize how artificial it is. Suppose, in the middle of a conversation about the weather, someone refers to God – perhaps saying something about God as the cause of the weather, or as answering prayers for a fine day. In many circles this would be deemed inappropriate; the person referring to God may be accused of 'bringing religion into' the discussion. If, instead, that person had referred to 30 degrees as the current temperature, nobody would have accused her of bringing mathematics into it; 30 degrees would have been a perfectly acceptable thing to mention. Why, then, is mentioning God less acceptable? The taboo, while not universal in western European society, is common. It is an artifice, which Muslims in particular find strange. It reveals a sensitivity to any hint of a revived religious authority. From a secular perspective religion not only lives in its own box, but the lid needs to be firmly in place.

Historically, the integrated account of reality was lost first. This, over time, made it possible to redescribe religion as a self-contained cultural phenomenon, irrelevant to the rest of society and its knowledge; and this in turn made it possible to think of God as unnecessary. Atheists may see this sequence of changes as real insights made possible by modern science. Others see them as historical accidents, motivated first by resistance to over-powerful church leaders, and later by excessive claims for the powers of the human mind.

Religious dogma

With its extreme claims for human knowledge, positivism persuaded large numbers of educated people, from the end of the eighteenth century until the 1960s, that the universe would be proved to be nothing but collections of atoms deterministically obeying eternal and impersonal laws of nature. This meant that God did not exist, religious practices like prayer and worship were meaningless and life after death was impossible; but it meant much more too. Since the theory counted humans as part of the deterministic universe, it implied that we have no free will; all our actions are caused by other events in an inescapable chain so that in theory, if we were able to know the exact state of every atom in the universe at a given point of time, it would be possible to predict its future for all time. Because, according to the theory, everything is determined, even our thoughts are not free. We think what we think because we are caused to do so: not only our freedom but all our values are mere creations of the human mind, not true qualities of reality. Whether these theories are true will be explored in later chapters.

The thought that God, the afterlife, freedom, values and morality were all erroneous inventions of the human brain inevitably generated strong reactions. Faced with such an emptying of the world, people looked to the churches to fill it up again. Church leaders responded in a variety of ways. Some remained confident that modern science would prove compatible with religious belief. Christian doctrines might need adapt-

> Faced with such an emptying of the world, people looked to the churches to fill it up again

ing in the light of new findings, but there was nothing unusual about that. This was the tradition which eventually came to be known as religious liberalism; the Churchmen's Union for the Advancement of Liberal Religious Thought, now known as Modern Church, was founded in 1898 to defend it.

The other responses were all reactionary. One was to defy modern reasoning processes in general. This stance now often claims the mantle of postmodernism. The argument runs that modernism, 'Enlightenment reason', believes in a single universally true account of reality, namely the one provided by modern western science, while in fact it is just one tradition among many and has no right to exalt its theories to the status of absolute truth.

The response which later came to be known as 'fundamentalism' accepted the logic of positivism but turned it on its head. Positivists argued that science has the facts and if the Bible disagrees with them the Bible is just plain wrong. Fundamentalists argued, and still argue, that the Bible has the facts and modern science is mere theory; if science disagrees with the Bible, science is just plain wrong. This tradition is now best known for its opposition to evolution.[11]

By far the most common response was a revived dualism along the lines of Descartes' philosophy, affirming a spiritual realm as well as a physical one. In this view science explains how the observable physical universe operates while religion explains the unobservable, the spiritual and our values. This led nineteenth-century churches to emphasize spiritual realities beyond the reach of science. Roman Catholics saw more visions of angels, saints and the Virgin Mary than they had seen since the Middle Ages. Evangelicals valued intense conversion experiences. Many rediscovered speaking in tongues, or the imminent second coming of Christ. Protestants and Catholics alike expected, and claimed to witness, more miracles; before then divine intervention had been considered a rare event, if it happened at all. The papacy insisted on accepting some very unlikely miracles and legends. At a more popular level more people saw ghosts. Modern Spiritualism, with its messages from the dead, was also established in the nineteenth century.[12]

These varying responses to the crisis of faith largely explain why Christian churches are the way they are today. Only the first, the 'liberal' response, takes a generally positive view of modern society's understandings of reality. From the perspective of the others the task of the Church is to resist the lure of secular society and cling on to its own distinctive teachings. In other words it has become the mirror image of militant atheism: with both sides agreeing that believing in God does not make sense, what divides them is whether to denounce religious belief in the name of reason or to denounce reason in the name of God.

For a while this negative attitude resulted in full churches; church life had far more vitality in the nineteenth century than in the eighteenth. Facing the threat of atheism, churches became popular by offering not a minor adaptation of modern secularism but a whole spiritual world independent of it. They therefore insisted that secular science had no business passing judgement on religious truths: religious truth-claims were to be justified in terms internal to religion. At the end of the nineteenth century the Roman Catholic hierarchy gave the word 'dogma' the meaning it now has. Originally derived from a Greek word meaning 'it seems', it came to mean (a) a divinely revealed truth, (b) proclaimed as such by solemn church teaching, and (c) binding on the faithful thereafter for ever.[13] In other words, in

> In reaction against the threat of science, believers came to value religious claims *because* they could not be rationally justified

21

reaction against the threat of science, believers came to value religious claims *because* they could not be rationally justified.

The pattern continues today. Some church leaders insist on factual claims about the distant past: Jesus was born of a virgin, walked on water and rose from the dead. Most people do not care whether any of this is true. If being a Christian is all about believing that certain unusual things happened thousands of years ago, why bother with it? Other beliefs demand a high price. If you are a Roman Catholic, using contraceptives is wrong. Some Protestant groups expect members to believe the world was made in six days about six thousand years ago. Various churches expect their members to take a strong line against abortion, assisted dying, alcohol, women in positions of leadership, same-sex partnerships and sex before marriage. This may seem a high price to pay for being a Christian; but many teach that there is an even higher price for not being one. God made Jesus suffer a cruel death by crucifixion in order to save the human race from eternal punishment in hell, but if you do not believe it you will go there anyway.

This is not typical of religious belief. When new religious beliefs arise, they do so for reasons. Every doctrine first appears when a person or a society thinks it is both true and important. The reasons are explored and debated. Critical questions get asked. Exactly what does it mean? In what circumstances does it apply, and when does it become irrelevant? When new challenges arise, should it be adapted to meet them? Over time, however, the original reasons cease to apply. Some doctrines then die out. Others survive because they are associated with a particular movement. They then become dogmas. Their new function is to be badges of identity, something you have to believe if you want to belong to that particular group.[14] Once this degeneration has taken place it becomes unacceptable to ask critical questions about the dogma: those who want to belong are expected just to accept it. Some people find this process attractive; assenting to beliefs which others find incredible can give a cheap sense of superiority. Today, though, it repels far more. The situation is exacerbated by the many church leaders who, mesmerized by the larger numbers of churchgoers

> Assenting to beliefs which others find incredible can give a cheap sense of superiority

in the nineteenth century, take that era as a model to be emulated. Dogmatism may have filled the churches in the nineteenth century, but over the last 50 years it has emptied them.

Society has moved on. The scientific threat to religion has now subsided. In the early twentieth century, from the time of Einstein and quantum theory, scientists began to realize that the universe is far more complex than they had previously thought. Most now accept that they cannot disprove the existence of God, freedom or values. Some theoretical physicists have been arguing that creation by a divine mind seems the best explanation of the way the universe works.

With the decline of atheism, more people are willing to admit to a desire for a spiritual dimension to their lives. Quite rightly, they expect their spirituality to make sense. At the very least this means it should be compatible with modern knowledge and values. In the following chapters I hope to show that the ordinary human experience of life makes better sense if we and the world are designed to relate to a divine mind.

2

Design

One of the most common claims of religious believers is that the world shows signs of intentional design. This chapter explores whether this is a legitimate reason for believing in a divine designer, or whether the appearances of design can be better explained in other ways.

In ancient and medieval times hardly anyone doubted it. They disagreed about which gods had created the world, how, and for what purpose, but nearly everyone thought it was intentionally designed.

As atheists have offered alternatives there have been three substantial debates. The first focuses on order and the laws of physics, the second on the way every species is adapted to its environment and the third on the fine tuning of physical laws. I shall not include the new American movement which calls itself 'intelligent design'. The aim of that movement is to deny evolution, and despite its name I think it functions as an interventionist argument rather than a design argument.

Order

First then the fact that the world seems ordered. The question of order is relevant to belief in God in two ways. One is whether the universe really is ordered. This will be the topic of Chapter 7. Here we will assume that it is ordered and ask whether its order has been designed.

Intentional design is a natural inference to make. The medieval scholar Thomas Aquinas described it as an analogy. When we observe that something is ordered we assume an intending mind has ordered it. In the same way, when we observe that the universe is ordered, we infer that it too must have been designed by a mind. Similarly, four centuries after Aquinas, Isaac Newton thought the motions of the heavenly bodies suggested a designer with a knowledge of mechanics: 'This most beautiful system of the sun, planets, and comets, could only proceed from the counsel and dominion of an intelligent and powerful being.'[1]

The first major critic of design was David Hume. Hume produced a number of arguments against divine design, some of which remain central to the continuing debate today. As noted in the last chapter, he was writing in the middle of the eighteenth century at a time when philosophers expected to establish truths with absolute certainty. Some had argued that the order in the world made the existence of a divine designer absolutely certain. Hume pointed out that order does not prove design. We see order in many situations but only in a minority do we know it is caused by an agent.[2]

More recently the idea of absolute certainty has been discredited. We now accept that certainty is not available, either in matters of religion or in any other matters; after all, you cannot prove with absolute certainty that this book exists. You may be dreaming, or enjoying the effects of the illegal substance you smoked this morning. Nevertheless we need to get on with our lives and

> The idea of absolute certainty has been discredited. We now accept that certainty is not available

make decisions, and we do so on the basis of what seems most likely to be true. Since scientific researchers characteristically describe their findings not as absolute certainties but as 'the best available hypotheses', the design argument, like all knowledge claims, nowadays works in a humbler mode. Philosophers still refer to design as one of the three traditional 'proofs' of the existence of God, though they no longer think they succeed as proofs. Hume was right to claim that the appearance of design does not make God's existence certain, but an intelligent divine being may still be the best available hypothesis to explain the universe as we know it.

Hume was writing at the beginning of the era which confidently expected science to explain reality without appealing to God. He made the point that when we deduce a cause from an effect, all we know about the cause is what the effect indicates. If the universe has indeed been created by God, this shows that God possesses the amount of power, intelligence and benevolence revealed in the universe but no more. He criticized theologians for assuming that they knew more about God than the design argument could establish; perhaps the universe was made by a committee of designers, or was a poor experiment in universe-making by an inferior god, or was created by a god who has lost interest in it and allows it to continue regardless of its condition until it breaks up with age. These remarks show how influential the dualism described in the last chapter had become. For thousands of years people had debated a wide range of questions about what the gods must be like, to explain why the world is the way it is. By Hume's time, dualism had produced a culture that excluded theology from all studies of the physical universe. As a result he could take for granted that the *only* relevance God could possibly have was to be its original creator. Before his time the argument would have seemed absurd.

Hume accepted Francis Bacon's theory that science should always work by induction from repeated observations. This means that scientists consider one thing the cause of another when we have observed that the effect follows the cause regularly. On this basis he argued that only if we could observe lots of universes, and notice that the ones governed by order are designed by God, could we infer that this one, being ordered, is probably also designed by God. Since, however, this universe is the only one we know about, we cannot appeal to any regularities. On this point, however, Bacon and Hume were mistaken. Scientists often develop theories about unique events, like the Big Bang.

Given our current understandings of knowledge and science, most of Hume's arguments no longer have the force they seemed to have in the eighteenth century. What remains significant is that there is no *proof*. When we reflect on the way the world is ordered, intentional design continues to be a popular inference; but perhaps we are being misled by appearances. Modern psychologists observe that seeing patterns enables us to process large amounts of information efficiently. This usually helps, but sometimes we mistakenly attribute patterns to random events. To infer that the world is designed may be a similar mistake. In that case, matter and the laws of nature just happen to be there, for no known reason. Their existence becomes a surd fact, one of those things science has to accept but cannot explain.

When we spell this out, it is an uncomfortable conclusion. Scientists usually dislike scientifically unexplainable facts; the whole point of science is to see what there is and find explanations for it. If the main reason for treating matter and the laws of nature as inexplicable is that the only alternative is to posit the existence of God, then perhaps the taboo on God is itself unscientific. Maybe the existence of God and the achievements of science are partners rather than competitors: either both are true, or neither is.

Biological adaptation

The appeal to biological adaptation is based on the rich diversity of species and organs, each apparently designed for its biological role. It was most popular from the seventeenth century to the nineteenth. At the time science was advancing rapidly, particularly in England, and in England it was often led by Church of England clergy.

Most of them were natural theologians who did not accept the dualist separation of the spiritual sphere from the physical. They stressed that the purpose of the world, and of human life, was to be found in the intentions of God. Those who did not believe in divine design were also enthusiastic about the new discoveries of science, but divine design could give those discoveries a seal of approval as God's plan for humanity.[3] What kept the argument popular was the countless new examples from the natural sciences, maintaining a sense of excitement about its wonders.

The first major work in this tradition, John Ray's *The Wisdom of God Manifested in the Works of Creation*, was published in 1691. Writing well before the idea of evolution had become popular, Ray believed that the earth and all its plants and animals had been created in their present form in the beginning, though he allowed for change through natural forces and human cultivation of the land.[4] The last and most influential of these works was William Paley's

Natural Theology (1802). When the evolution debate broke out, it was Paley's work which provided the background against which evolutionists reacted.

Paley wrote his book about 50 years after Hume and 50 before Darwin. His critics today think he was behind the times, using arguments which Hume had already refuted, and which Darwin would well and truly bury. I think this is unfair to him. He did take for granted the science of his day, and this meant accepting that the world was only a few thousand years old and all the species alive in his day had been there from the beginning. Nevertheless the idea of evolution was around; both Hume and Paley knew of it, though in their days there was very little research data to justify it.

Most of Paley's work, like that of earlier natural theologians, piles up illustrations from the sciences to illustrate divine design. The key arguments are expressed in his watch analogy:

> In crossing a heath, suppose I pitched my foot against a *stone*, and were asked how the stone came to be there, I might possibly answer, that, for any thing I knew to the contrary, it had lain there for ever; nor would it perhaps be very easy to show the absurdity of this answer. But suppose I had found a *watch* upon the ground, and it should be enquired how the watch happened to be in that place, I should hardly think of the answer which I had before given, that, for any thing I knew, the watch might have always been there. Yet why should not this answer serve for the watch, as well as for the stone? ... [Because] its several parts are framed and put together for a purpose, e.g. that they are so formed and adjusted as to produce motion.[5]

There must therefore have been an intelligent maker. Aware of the usual objections to the analogy, he then argued that our inference to a watchmaker would not be invalidated in any of the following cases: if we had never seen a watch made, known anybody capable of making one, or understood how it was made; if the watch sometimes went wrong; if it contained parts whose use seemed incomprehensible or superfluous; if somebody pointed out that if it had not been there something else would have been there with another unusual combination of materials (a point discussed below with respect to fine tuning); if it were argued that the watch were nothing but the result of the laws of metallic nature (the point already noted about what the laws of nature are); if it were argued that the observer did not know about the matter. Finding the watch, as described, would be enough information to infer a watchmaker. All these points appeal to the signs of design in the way the world is ordered, and are still pertinent to the debate.

For us today the critical question is whether evolution can account for the appearances of design in such a way that we no longer need to infer God. By Paley's time scientific discoveries had already elaborated laws by which one event was caused by another, or one plant or animal created by its parents, and atheists were already using them as a way of dispensing with God. Paley replied that indirect causation does not in any way dispense with the need for an intelligent designer; if the discoverer of the watch found that, as well as being able to tell the time, it contained within it a mechanism which could create new watches like itself, this would increase our admiration of the machine rather than reduce it. After Darwin published his *Origin of Species*, Frederick Temple, later to become Archbishop of Canterbury, extended Paley's point to refer specifically to evolution: if the watch proved able to create *better* watches than itself, that too would be evidence of design.

> The critical question is whether evolution can account for the appearances of design in such a way that we no longer need to infer God

We can all agree with Paley this far: *if* what we see in the watch implies design by an intelligent being, then we infer an intelligent designer. Furthermore, *how* the designer set about manufacturing it – whether directly or by means of a watch-making watch – is irrelevant to the main point. However it is precisely design by an intelligent being which atheists today deny.

The atheism of Paley's day was different from ours. The eighteenth century had been gripped by excitement with the new sciences and their power to uncover the mysteries of the universe. If anybody denied the wonder of it all, it was conservative theologians with their warnings about the Fall and the wrath of God. Atheists agreed with Paley that the world was wonderfully intricate and seemed to be astonishingly well designed. Against that kind of atheism it made good sense for Paley to insist that design implies a designer. During the nineteenth century, however, atheism changed – perhaps partly in response to Paley's arguments, though there were other reasons. Later atheists *denied* that they perceived any evidence of design in the world. To be consistent about their atheism, they suppressed their sense of wonder and learned to evaluate whatever scientists discovered as 'nothing but' a development from, or adaptation of, something else. Against this newer atheism, Paley's analogy is powerless.

Charles Darwin's *Origin of Species* (1859) made evolution more credible by producing much more research data and by proposing a means, namely natural selection. There are two main implications for the design argument. The first is that it makes possible a God-free account of how living beings developed into the rich array we have. Sometimes Darwin wrote that his account refuted the design argument: 'We can no longer argue that, for instance, the beautiful hinge of a bivalve shell must have been made by an intelligent being.'[6] His achievement, however, was to describe a process which would make sense even if God did not exist. In other words the appearance of design does not *necessarily* imply the existence of God. Richard Dawkins has suggested that Darwin made it possible for the first time to be an intellectually fulfilled atheist.[7]

The point is often exaggerated. Evolution describes the process by which the bivalve shell developed into what it is, quite independently of whether it was designed by God. It may be a naturalistic process in a godless world, as atheists believe; but the evidence makes it equally possible that it was God's process for producing the bivalve shell with its hinge, or alternatively God's way of giving living beings freedom to produce whatever they will. Neither Darwin's data nor the theory of natural selection offer any way to choose between these three possibilities. We can look at the hinge of a bivalve shell, accepting that it evolved, and still ask ourselves which of the three is most likely to have produced something like that. On this question many would still agree with Paley.

Darwin also drew attention to the large amount of waste and suffering. The natural theologians, by contrast, had emphasized the goodness of nature. On this point Darwin was heavily influenced by Malthus' theory of populations, and stressed how organic life is a constant struggle for existence: 'I cannot persuade myself that a beneficent and omnipotent God would have designedly created the Ichneumonidae with the express intention of their feeding within the live bodies of Caterpillars, or that a cat should play with mice.'[8]

Here the difference between the two is that they both see the same things, and Paley infers benevolent design while Darwin does not. This remains the situation today. We see the same processes in nature, but some of us are impressed by the glory, wonder and purposeful design of it all while others are not impressed at all. Both responses are possible.

Fine tuning

The theory of fine tuning is a twentieth-century development. Theoretical physicists have shown that life would have been impossible if the laws of nature had been the tiniest amount different from what they are.

There are a number of critical variables in the way the universe works. One is the size of the explosion in the Big Bang: if it had differed by one part in 10^{60} this universe could not have existed.[9] Others are the distribution of gas in the universe, the weight of neutrinos, the total mass of the universe, the force of gravity, the force of electromagnetism, the strong nuclear force, weak interaction and the temperature of the interiors of hot stars. The slightest deviation in any of these values, and life would have been impossible. They were all established within the first fraction of a second after the Big Bang.

Given the figures, many scientists find it overwhelmingly improbable that chance would have produced what we have; a divine power must have been at work.[10] Others argue that the inference is not valid. It assumes that the enormous range of possible initial states of the universe are all equally unlikely to happen. We do not know that they were all equally unlikely; in order to know that, we would have to know about the process which caused the Big Bang, and we do not.

> Many scientists find it overwhelmingly improbable that chance would have produced what we have; a divine power must have been at work

Perhaps all the other possibilities were less likely, for reasons we do not know. This, however, is a big 'perhaps', entirely dependent on our ignorance.

Another argument is that we are looking at it from our biased human perspective. The only Big Bang we know about produced laws of physics which made our lives possible. We think that alternatives, in which life was impossible, would have been disappointing, because we attribute meaning to the life we know about.

A more popular argument, known as the multiverse theory, is that there must be many universes. Scientists debate this proposal at length. Some think it is a pointless idea: there is no evidence that other universes exist, and even if they do, the life-permitting character of this universe still needs explaining.[11] Others think the life-permitting character of our universe becomes less surprising if it is one of many. If we accept this idea we seem to be faced with a choice between two possible explanations. Either our universe is one of many billions (and this one would have to be our home because we probably could not exist in the others) or this universe has been designed by an intelligent mind. Which of the two should we prefer?

> Either our universe is one of many billions ... or this universe has been designed by an intelligent mind

Usually when scientists look for explanations Ockham's razor is a useful guide: when in doubt, go for the simplest explanation and do not posit the existence of anything unnecessary. It has been applied to fine tuning in two ways. One is: in the absence of any divine mind directing the process, would a simpler universe be more likely to exist than a more complex one such as ours? Or do we just assume that simpler things are more probable because our brains find them easier to understand?[12] The other is: if we have to choose between creation by God and billions of universes, which is the simpler explanation? Richard Dawkins argues that invoking a divine being to explain the complexity of the universe, far from solving the problem, makes it harder because God, as the creator, would have to be even more complex; we would then have to explain how God came to exist.[13] Whether God's existence would need to be explained in such a way will be discussed in Chapter 6; we can see Dawkins' point that God would have to be extremely complex. However, the multiverse theory would be extremely complex too. If behind the Big Bang lies yet another process producing billions of universes, then we need to ask what produced the universe-producing process; and whatever answer we find, it remains to ask what produced *that*. We seem to be postulating a regress with no foreseeable end point.

Others reply that the multiverse theory is an extreme case of multiplying entities in order to avoid the obvious conclusion. Believers can add that there are other reasons, like the ones explored elsewhere in this book, for believing in God. If there is a God, of course, God may have created any number of other universes in addition to this one; but if the only reason for positing many universes is a determination to dispense with God, then the determination to dispense with God begins to look like an unscientific refusal to face the evidence.

Conclusion

To summarize, all versions of the design argument appeal to some aspect of the universe which seems most easily explained as intended design. In each case it is possible to argue that there was no design, and that we only perceive design because of the way in which humans think.

Denying design produces two issues. One is the limits of science. It may seem that the appearances of design are explained by the laws of nature, but as we have seen the laws of nature only describe regularities; they do not explain what causes them. What *would* be a God-free explanation of the appearances of design would be a convincing theory about what causes the laws of nature to be the way they are. Given the current state of scientific research it seems most unlikely that such a theory will ever be developed. Lacking any explanation of this kind, we have to accept that we have reached the limits of science. Yet the limit is an uncomfortable place for scientists to be. It is in the nature of science to ask why things are the way they are. If the only available answer is that we just do not know, then the hypothesis of design by God should be judged on its merits, not ruled out on principle.

The other issue is the difficulty of dispensing with all ideas of design. If the world has not been designed, it only seems designed because imagining design gives humans some kind of evolutionary advantage. If cause and effect is the only explanation there is, and we are to strip away all design from the way we see the world, it will be bleaker and emptier than most of us would find comfortable. It is possible to conceive of reality without any design and we can, if we so choose, train our minds to see it this way. If we do, reality becomes just one pointless event after another and denying the existence of God reinforces our sense that we are not missing anything.

Another possibility is to believe that our lives and the world around us witness to some kind of intention behind everything. We may feel pulled into a relationship with it. If we have feelings of this kind, believing in God is a way to make sense of them.

The difference between the two is extreme. On one account reality witnesses to an intending mind that transcends human minds, with purposes that transcend human purposes. The world around us, and our own lives, are full of significance greater than we can understand. On the other account reality consists of unintending, impersonal, purposeless processes which only take place because there is a tendency, so far unexplained, for things to move in regular ways. To believe this is to empty the universe of everything except matter and those processes.

It is not surprising that many atheists seek a middle way between these two extremes, so that they can still admire the intricacy, beauty and potential around us while denying divine design. Tempting though it seems, however, there is no such middle way. Every attempt to create one has to explain what it is that is being admired. To admire impersonal processes that are devoid of mental capacities makes no more sense than admiring the number 4 for coming between 3 and 5. This is why many atheists end up treating evolution or the laws of nature as though they had intentions – admiring them for their achievements, trusting them to continue doing what they have done so far – in other words, treating them as gods.

The justifiable options are the extreme ones. As a logical argument, divine design can be neither proved nor disproved. What is at issue is whether it is the best explanation we have of reality as we experience it. It is our experience of life, rather than the arguments, that is likely to point us in one direction or the other.

To believe the universe was designed is to attribute to it an intention, a purpose. Intention and purpose are only possible where there are values. In the next chapter we turn to the question of what we mean by the values we hold, and what they imply about God.

3

Values

——•◆•——

*If I had to die now, I would say: 'Was that all?' And: 'That is not really
how I understood it.' And: 'It was rather noisy.'*

(Jewish writer in Berlin, who took his own life
in 1935 in despair at the successes of the Nazis)[1]

Some people reject God because they reject the values they associate
with God. Others see God as the essential ground of their values. My
aim in this chapter is to show that if we are to make any sense of our
values, we need to presuppose a higher evaluating mind something
like God.

Science does not find values. Some people conclude that there are
no values in the world, so we have to explain why people invent them.
Others conclude that they do exist, independently of human inventions,
so we have to explain how we can distinguish true from false values.

Although it can be confusing I shall follow tradition by using the word
'value' in two senses. In the more general sense it covers not only
'value' in the narrower sense, but all our value concepts including
progress, purpose, beauty, meaning and morality. This wider sense of
'values' is the topic of this chapter and the next, and I describe what
they have in common at the end of this chapter. In its narrower sense
'value' refers specifically to our concept that some things are valuable,
and is described in this chapter after progress and purpose and before
meaning. The pattern will be that progress presupposes purpose, purpose
presupposes value and value presupposes meaning.

Progress

Progress is change towards desired objectives. We all have problems
we would like to solve, hopes and ambitions we would like to achieve.

Without a desired objective – a purpose – there is only change, not progress.

We talk about progress for individuals, families, communities, nations and the world. To be credible, our ideas of progress need to be consistent with each other: our hopes for ourselves have to be consistent with any hopes we have for our families and local communities. If we want to make the world a better place, our hopes for the world will need to be consistent with our hopes for those closer to us. This means that, unless we are very self-centred, our hopes for our own progress are part of a bigger vision of progress.

In Europe enthusiasm for progress reached its peak in the eighteenth and nineteenth centuries.[2] People expected progress to occur in various ways. We have inherited their ideas of progress through scientific research, education, economic growth and new technologies. They also had other ideas which we have not inherited, like racial progress through killing off 'inferior' races and filling the world with white Europeans, or persuading the 'lower classes' to have fewer children so that future generations would be of 'better stock'.

We cannot have a concept of world progress unless we have a concept of humanity as a unity. The ancient Stoics thought of humanity as a unity but it was Christianity that gave the concept a theoretical basis by claiming that we were all created by a single God with a consistent set of purposes. On this basis it made sense to believe that world humanity really can make progress towards fulfilling God's plans. Not that Christianity did always expect progress in this world, but the idea was revived in the seventeenth century.

By the end of the nineteenth century it was no longer scientifically acceptable to interpret progress in terms of God's plans. Enthusiasts for progress replaced God with other unifying principles like Providence and Destiny. When we ask what these terms meant it is difficult to pin them down; either they were another word for God or they seem to have been an appeal to fatalism or determinism. The most influential replacement for God was scientific Necessity. Many believed that the laws of nature included laws of human progress, so that progress was bound to happen. Thus Karl Marx thought the 'dictatorship of the proletariat' was inevitable.

These replacements changed the character of progress. Instead of being pulled towards a vision of God's plan, progress was pushed by inevitable scientific laws. However, inevitable scientific laws do not desire objectives. All that remained was change, and change imposed by laws of nature is not necessarily change for the better. By and large this is our present situation. The eighteenth and nineteenth centuries generated many challenging new ideas about progress. The twentieth produced virtually none: it just followed through the logical implications of the ones it had inherited. Concentrating our means of progress on economic growth and new technologies, we have become better and better at achieving certain objectives; but, lacking a coherent theory of purpose, we have lost the ability to think through which objectives are worth achieving. We have become like hikers whose map has been blown away by the wind: we no longer know which way to go, so we carry on the way we were going before.

> We have become better and better at achieving certain objectives; but we have lost the ability to think through which objectives are worth achieving

This is mainly because once God is taken out of the picture the main reason for seeing humanity as a unity has gone; all that remains is different people with different values. The 1948 International Declaration of Human Rights attempted to establish universal truths about humans in the hope that if every country could agree on a set of principles, they would provide a basis for resolving international disagreements. Some countries rejected it as a western concept. Some postmodernists argue against internationalism in general; if we cannot assume that other people's interests are compatible with our interests, it seems we should expect our governments to defend our own nation's interests without caring about the effects on other people.

Purpose

Progress therefore needs a desired objective, a purpose to aim for. The problem that arose with progress in the nineteenth century had in a sense already arisen with purpose. The ancient philosopher Aristotle thought we could explain the way things are in terms of four causes. Three of the causes are still accepted today; there is the stuff a thing is made of, how that stuff is arranged, and what causes it to change and develop. The fourth type of cause, final causes, was the one early modern scientists rejected.

For Aristotle, the final cause of a thing is the objective towards which it moves. The final cause of an acorn is to become an oak tree.[3] Aristotle thought final causes were internal to each thing. They were not really purposes because he was not saying acorns *want* to become oak trees. However, when medieval Christians rediscovered Aristotle they thought final causes could be God's purposes. Early modern scientists accepted God's purposes but argued that Aristotle's final causes did not really explain anything. Later, when God was taken out of the scientific picture, scientists saw it as their task to explain the processes of nature without reference to any future objectives at all.

In practice scientists use the language of purpose all the time. If we ask why some plants produce pretty, scented flowers, the answer is that they do it to attract bees. If we ask why we have kidneys, the answer is that they purify the blood. However, for those who do not believe

> From an atheist perspective, kidneys do not have a purpose at all

in God this language of purpose is only shorthand for saying the thing evolved like that because this is how it survived. Strictly speaking, from an atheist perspective, kidneys do not have a purpose at all; they exist simply because they enable the animal they are in to survive.

If there is no God, the only purposes that remain are the ones humans create. Some purposes are pure self-gratification with an end point. Tonight I shall get drunk. Tomorrow I shall feel awful but tonight it will be great. Most of us have other purposes beyond self-gratification. The question is how to make sense of them.

Suppose a young friend of yours comes to you and says, 'I don't think my life has any purpose. I've decided to commit suicide.' How will you respond? If there is no God, the usual account is that your friend is absolutely right: nobody's life has any purpose. After the Big Bang the unthinking and impersonal elements of the universe obeyed equally unthinking and impersonal laws of nature, eventually producing human beings with the capacity to invent purposes for their lives. In that case the correct response to your friend would be to say,

'You are quite right. Your life does not have any purpose given to you. So you could commit suicide, or alternatively you could dream up a purpose for your life, just so as to give yourself the feeling that your life has a purpose. It's up to you which to choose.'

At less critical times many people do claim to hold this view; but, faced with the prospect of a life-or-death decision based on it, I doubt whether anyone would take it so seriously. It is even difficult to imagine someone going halfway and saying something like, 'I don't know whether your life has a point or not. Look it up on the internet.'

> 'I don't know whether your life has a point or not. Look it up on the internet'

Far more likely, you would say something like, 'You mustn't think of killing yourself. *Of course* your life has a purpose.'

If you said that, would you really believe it? How would you claim to know? Could you offer reasons? If not, either you are just lying – in effect, saying what you think people say on these occasions, without worrying about whether there is any truth in it – or you are responding to a gut instinct deep down within you, telling you that everybody's life has a purpose.

You may think up some arguments, like 'Your children need you'; but your friend is in a better position to judge those than you are. Ultimately, to say that a person's life has a purpose over and above any purpose that person creates for himself is to locate it within a bigger picture, implying that the bigger picture has a bigger purpose.

This is typical of the way we normally think. If I ask you, 'For what purpose are you revising for your examinations?' You might answer, 'Because I want to get a degree.' 'For what purpose do you want a degree?' 'Because I want to become an accountant.' 'Why do you want to become an accountant?' If I keep asking we shall eventually reach a future point that you have not thought about yet; but until we reach that point the answers you give will locate your present purpose within a bigger story of purposes.

If every big picture only makes sense within an even bigger picture, is there a 'biggest picture' incorporating all the others? If so, what is the purpose of that? If we can explain the purpose of this 'biggest picture' within the context of something even bigger, then it is no longer the biggest picture.

There seem to be only two options. One is that our big pictures do not represent reality; they are really only illusory attempts to justify the individual purposes we have invented for ourselves. In this case there are no right answers, conflict between different purposes is inevitable, and nobody has any business decreeing a purpose for somebody else's life. If a person does not create a purpose for her own life, she may as well commit suicide.

The other option is that there are real purposes contained within a real big picture, but the biggest picture is beyond the reach of ordinary human minds. In this case there are two roles for our big pictures: they can guide our sense of purpose here and now, but they also draw our attention to the existence of a dimension beyond human understanding. That dimension will have to include a purposing mind.

Value

Purpose implies value. The purposes we have reveal what we think would be a valuable thing to achieve. So what is value?

The usual classification distinguishes between intrinsic value, in which a thing is valuable because of its own nature, and instrumental value, in which a thing is valuable as a means to something else: if music is intrinsically valuable, a piano has instrumental value. The most common view is that instrumental value is explained by its relation to intrinsic value, so it is intrinsic value which is of interest here.

Intrinsic value can be understood as either subjective or objective. A subjective account of value claims that when we describe something as valuable, all we are saying is that some people have certain kinds of feelings about it. An objective account claims that a thing is valuable whether or not any humans value it: calling it valuable makes a truth claim about it over and above our feelings. It is this difference which relates to our question about God. Are there any objective intrinsic values, and if there are, can we explain them without appealing to God?

John Mackie's 'queerness' argument is a good account of the case against objective value. He applied queerness in two ways: to what values would be, and to how we would know about them. On what they would be he said that they would be 'utterly different from anything else in the universe'. On how we would know about them he said 'it would have to be by some special faculty of moral perception or intuition, utterly different from our ordinary ways of knowing everything else'. He found this unsatisfactory:

> None of our ordinary accounts of sensory perception or introspection or the framing and confirming of explanatory hypotheses or inference or logical construction or conceptual analysis, or any combination of these, will provide a satisfactory answer: 'a special sort of intuition' is a lame answer, but it is the one to which the clear-headed objectivist is compelled to resort.[4]

Critics reply that Mackie was merely revealing his positivist presuppositions, assuming that nothing exists unless it can be deduced or perceived with the senses.[5] In reality what we think we know is based on a much wider range of sources. According to Darwinian theory intuition was established in our evolutionary history millions of years before the conscious logical processes Mackie describes. Rational analysis, far from being self-sufficient, is an addition to, and depends upon, other processes like intuition, instinct and imagination; it cannot replace them. This does not mean their revelations are always true – there is a proper place for rational analysis to interrogate them – but far from being queer, they are essential features of our normal understanding.

Rational analysis, far from being self-sufficient, is an addition to, and depends upon, other processes like intuition, instinct and imagination

If all values are subjective, nothing is of value unless at least one person values it. In some cases this makes sense: if there is a television programme that absolutely nobody watches, perhaps it has no value. In other cases it produces unexpected results. Very few people consciously value bacteria, yet our lives depend on them. Dinosaur bones have immense value because they generate endless fascination: but when the dinosaurs were alive there were no humans to value them, so the theory denies that they had any value then.

Mackie accepted that most of us, when we talk about values, think of them as objective:[6] when we declare something valuable we think we are saying more than just that some people happen to value it. Nevertheless, just as there is no purpose without a purposing mind, it is difficult to conceive what it would mean to say something is valuable, if no mind capable of evaluating were ever to value it. To say something is valuable even when no humans value it is to say that it is still valuable, and this in turn implies that some mind or other is still valuing it. This brings us to the question: do only humans evaluate, or is there a higher mind that evaluates more authoritatively than humans do?

This superhuman evaluator could be society. Many people accept the values of their host society. On the other hand there is always a good number of people who think their society's values are wrong: not just wrong for individuals who have chosen different values for themselves, but objectively wrong. If we think that society's values are objectively wrong, we need to appeal to a higher authority, a more authoritative evaluator, than society.

Meaning

To value something is to attribute to it a meaning which is significant to us. Value presupposes meaning. At its most basic, 'meaning' signifies: so the word 'three' means a number between two and four. Sometimes actions or situations mean things in a similar way. When you say, 'I give you this ring as a sign of our marriage,' it is not just the words which have meaning: it is the action in a particular setting. In ways like this, to describe an event or activity as 'meaningful' is to say it has a quality which resonates with our deep concerns.

As with purpose and value, it helps if the things we find most meaningful are consistent with each other and express our presuppositions about the meaning of our life as a whole. As well as the meanings of words and the meanings of actions we sometimes talk about our lives having meaning. Douglas Adams' joke about the meaning of life being 42 resonates because we know instinctively that the meaning of our lives cannot be reduced to a number. It cannot be measured. We cannot define it.

Many people deny that there is any particular meaning given to our lives. We create whatever meanings our lives have. In the nineteenth century Nietzsche wrote: 'Ultimately man finds in things nothing but what he himself has imported into them: the finding we call science, the importing – art, religion, love, pride.'[7] In 1981 Richard Rorty wrote: 'there is nothing deep down inside us except what we have put there ourselves, no criterion that we have not created in the course of creating a practice, no standard of rationality that is not an appeal to such a criterion, no rigorous argumentation that is not obedience to our own conventions.'[8]

People who argue like this nearly always expect us to create our own meanings. On this account, if you feel your life is meaningful, this is all the meaning you can expect to have: so to say your life is meaningful is just to describe a feeling.

Most of us want to say more than this about the meaning of our lives. Robert Nozick illustrated the problem with an 'experience machine'. We wire your brain up to a machine which can produce in your mind any experience you want. You can spend the rest of your life having whatever experiences you like. It has not been invented yet, but if it was, the question is: would you use it? Nozick says: 'We learn that something matters to us in addition to experience by imagining an experience machine and then realising that we would not use it.'[9] John Cottingham argues:

> to count towards the meaningfulness of a life these varied activities [activities we find meaningful] have to be more than just performed by the agent with an eye to personal satisfaction; they have to be capable of being informed by a vision of their value in the whole, by a sense of the worthwhile part they play in the growth and flowering of each unique human individual, and of the other human lives with which that story is necessarily interwoven.[10]

You may like to reflect on whether this is true of your life.

Values in general

Having introduced progress, purpose, value and meaning, I shall now make some general observations about all four. There are two things they all have in common. First, they only work in connection with consciousness. They can only exist where some conscious mind houses them. Second, science does not explain them. It presupposes them – it would be impossible to engage in any search for knowledge without some values and some sense of purpose and progress – but values are not what science itself reveals.

When people started thinking that values are pure human invention, they thought the implications were massive. In 1919 Bertrand Russell wrote:

> That Man is the product of causes which had no prevision of the end they were achieving; that his origin, his growth, his hopes and fears, his loves and his beliefs, are but the outcome of accidental collocations of atoms . . . that all the labours of the ages, all the devotion, all the inspiration, all the noonday brightness of human genius, are destined to extinction in the vast death of the solar system . . . all these things, if not quite beyond dispute, are yet so nearly certain, that no philosophy which rejects them can hope to stand. Only within the scaffolding of these truths, only on the firm foundation of unyielding despair, can the soul's habitation henceforth be safely built.[11]

All the devotion, all the inspiration, all the noonday brightness of human genius, are destined to extinction in the vast death of the solar system

Today a more common position is that although there are no objective values in the world, we create our own. If there is no God, this is the only possible way to have any. Daniel Dennett has proposed a detailed description of how evolution caused us to create meanings for our lives.[12] Some people think this is all we should expect our values to be. Others make the following criticisms.

Must we create values, or is it just that we happen to do so?

To say 'there are no values so we must create our own values' is even less defensible than saying 'there are no shufflegruffles so we must create our own shufflegruffles'. There is no imperative to create shufflegruffles, and if we did they would be no more or less than what we chose to create. Nevertheless, it is logically possible that an imperative to create shufflegruffles might arise one day. In the case of values, on the other hand, even that logical possibility is unavailable: until such time as we have values, there cannot be any imperatives at all.

An alternative is to focus on the processes by which humans create values, from a comparatively dispassionate perspective, explaining how, as a matter of fact, humans do create values even though we do not need to. I do not know of anyone who manages to be completely dispassionate about it: not even Nietzsche and Russell were.

Instead, people who believe we create our own values enthuse about it. They say things like, 'We must create our own values'; they think their way of creating values is 'better' than the other options. This of course is nonsense: according to the theory we do not have any values until we have created some for ourselves, so there is nothing we must do and there is no best anything. What such people are really doing is proposing to develop values on the basis of values they already hold; but to admit as much would contradict the whole idea that we create our own values.

Self-created values are arbitrary

For a moment let us imagine that you wake up one morning valuing absolutely nothing and decide to create some values. It would be a difficult thing to do; if you really were completely devoid of values you would have no reason to create any. You could not tell yourself that it would be a good idea to create values, because 'good' is a value. This means that if you did go through this experience and create some values, those values would be arbitrary.

Self-created values would be a complete fiction

Suppose you start from scratch and decide to count your life as valuable. You then count your friends, your Facebook account and your dog as valuable. You instruct yourself to behave as though they were valuable. This process does not change the universe. It only changes the attitudes in your mind. Some bits of the universe now seem valuable to you because you have decided so to perceive them, and for no other reason. You have created a fiction.

Self-created values misinterpret how individuals relate to society

Of course nobody really thinks that people do create values from scratch like this. We are brought up in societies, we inherit values from them, most of us accept them, some of us question them and a few succeed in changing them. However, this means that we do not create values. Individuals and societies alike inherit values. We may change them, but we change them in the light of the values we hold at the time, values given to us by a tradition which itself never started from scratch with a blank sheet.

Self-created values lead to lack of commitment

Even if it is society rather than individuals that creates values, it is you as an individual who decides which values to accept. Tomorrow you may decide to change them. Today you can be a suicide bomber for the Taliban, tomorrow you can give it all up to be a steam engine fanatic. You could decide to value consistency; but that too would be your own decision, and you may

> You could decide to value consistency; but that too would be your own decision, and you may abandon it tomorrow

abandon it tomorrow. As long as our values are the product of our own will, they are subordinate to our will. The authority structure is always the wrong way round: values can never give direction to our lives, because we have given them their direction. We end up as classic postliberals, refusing to be committed to anything.

Self-created values become true by definition

If all values are human creations, with no authority above us to declare our evaluations right or wrong, then each person's values are the right values by definition. If the US government thinks it was right to send troops to Afghanistan, then their judgement was correct – for the US government. For many Afghans, on the other hand, it was the wrong thing to do, and that judgement is also correct – for those Afghans.

Self-created values cannot resolve conflict

If all values are created by individuals and societies, so that no values are right or wrong except from one perspective or another, we have no reason to expect any progress towards resolving our value disagreements. We can only expect that just as disagreements about values have always caused wars, they will continue to do so.

Conclusion

Few atheists today appreciate the full implications of the denial of objective values. Nietzsche did, and Russell's argument quoted above comes close to Nietzsche's position; but today the rhetoric of 'creating our own values' gives the impression that nothing important is lost by such a denial. To take an example, one of the commonest arguments against believing in God is that it is incompatible with all the evil and suffering in the world. However, what counts for values also counts for disvalues, the things we dislike or disapprove of. If we create our own values, to speak of evil in the world can only mean that we have chosen to count some things as evil, and suffering is only objectionable because we have decided to call it objectionable. In real life, of course, people who are in great pain do not *decide* to count it as a disvalue; they experience it as such despite a preference not to.

The idea that all values are human creations was the product of positivism. Positivism starts with the fact that science cannot prove the existence of values, and deduces that therefore there are no values unless we create them. The alternative is to start the other way round: we all experience values all the time, so since science cannot explain them we need some other account of them.

Thomas Aquinas argued that by reflecting on the finite things of the physical world the human mind is able to know something of what lies beyond – the things on which finite things depend.[13] This is a good description of how scientific research normally works: we start with established data and theories which convince us, we examine them, and this leads us to develop new hypotheses about new entities. However, Aquinas believed that this process can lead us to knowledge about God. Today, science often proceeds from knowledge of observables to hypotheses about unobservables, but is restricted by the taboo on any reference to religious entities like God. Aquinas lived long before this taboo had been invented, and it seemed to him a perfectly natural connection to make. As John Cottingham has put it recently, there is 'a perpetual tension in our make-up: we are constrained by our nature, but we see beyond it ... The human condition is paradoxical precisely because it is our nature, qua human beings, to have boundless aspirations which we cannot, qua human beings, fulfil.'[14]

So how do we explain our values? This chapter indicates two persistent features. First, our concepts of progress, purpose, value and meaning usually focus on local and personal matters, but they only have the quality they do if they can be understood within a wider setting; and that wider setting likewise can only have its quality if it is understood within a wider setting still. Even though we usually do not think about it, there has to be a big picture underlying all our values; otherwise they would be arbitrary and conflict with each other.

How big does the big picture have to be? When we reflect on it, it makes no sense to think any part of the universe is valuable unless the universe as a whole is valuable. This raises the question: what do we mean by calling the universe valuable? Since the idea is not self-explanatory, does the value of the universe also need to be explained in terms of another value bigger still? It seems to me that it does. Our understanding of values is always incomplete. We start with our ordinary awareness that life happens to be full of values, and when we try to explain these values our explanations keep directing our attention further and further away from our own little selves towards something bigger than the human mind can conceive.

The second feature our values have in common is that they can only be values by relating to a conscious evaluating mind. If the values we hold are indeed part of a bigger picture of value, there must be a bigger mind that does that bigger valuing, something with an overall view of the universe.

There remain two options. One is that values are figments of the human imagination, so that nothing has value over and above what we choose to consider valuable. The other is that our values are part of a bigger story of values; and if we follow the implications, we have to root them in values and an evaluator that transcend human understanding. As in the case of design, the coherent options are the extreme ones. The idea of a middle way, affirming values without God, merely claims for a godless world qualities that can only exist in relation to God.

Values

The human experience of values is one of the main reasons why most of the world's population believe in some kind of divine being. For most people it is just a gut feeling, not a logical argument. I have tried to show that, in addition to gut feelings, it makes sense.

4

Morality

————·•◆•·————

'If God is dead, everything is permitted,' declares Ivan in Dostoevsky's 1880 novel *The Brothers Karamazov.*

I believe this judgement is basically correct. My argument will be similar to the argument about values, in that if morality is a human creation it cannot do the work we normally expect it to do. The question is not whether atheists can live equally good moral lives – of course they often do – but how to *justify* our moral standards. Do they make sense?

Without God, there is nobody with authority to forbid anything. The moral rules must have been created by humans, so why should *I* obey *your* moral rules? The only coherent accounts are the extreme ones: either morality is just a human technique for manipulating each other, or it expresses real qualities which can only be explained in terms of a being more authoritative than other humans.

Alastair MacIntyre offered a controversial interpretation of the story about Captain Cook and his crew exploring Polynesia. They were astonished to find that the Polynesians had extremely liberal sexual habits. On the other hand, at meal times they had a very strict rule that women and men were not to eat together. When the Europeans asked why, their answer bequeathed a new word to the English language: taboo.

The Europeans asked what 'taboo' meant, but did not receive a satisfactory answer. Did 'taboo' mean 'prohibited'? No: it was prohibited *because* it was taboo; but the Polynesians could not explain why they refused to perform a taboo act. It seems that they themselves did not really understand what they meant, and this conclusion was reinforced by the fact that 40 years later the taboos were abolished and nobody seemed to mind.[1]

Anthropologists now tell us this often happens, and they explain it historically. The Europeans had arrived at a time when an old tradition was breaking down. At an earlier stage the rules had been part of a wider account, explaining how and why the gods had created them, and how they should therefore behave. When the Europeans arrived the reasons for the obligations had been rejected and then forgotten, but some of the practices still survived.

This pattern is well researched. What is controversial is MacIntyre's claim: that the same decline has taken place in modern western society. The argument is that medieval Christianity had a comparatively coherent account of how humanity relates to God and the world, and this provided a basis for the moral rules. After the Reformation there was no longer any agreement about God, so moralists set about establishing independent accounts of morality. MacIntyre describes rights, duties, utilitarianism, social contracts, intuitionism and other moral theories as the flotsam and jetsam left over after the shipwreck of a coherent moral system. Previously morality had worked with three concepts: humanity as it is, humanity as it would be if it realized its full potential, and the means to get from one to the other. The post-Enlightenment theories omit the concept of humanity as it would be if it realized its full potential, retaining only humanity as it is and a list of rules. This leaves us wondering why we ought to obey the rules.[2]

> The post-Enlightenment theories omit the concept of humanity as it would be if it realized its full potential, retaining only humanity as it is and a list of rules

So far I agree with MacIntyre. However, whereas his response was to argue for virtue ethics, mine is to reclaim the role of God. I shall briefly introduce the main moral authorities and ask two questions of each: how do we find out which moral commands it gives us, and why should we obey them? I shall start with the replacements most similar to God, objective universal authorities, then move on to socially constructed moralities, individualist moralities, and emotivism. Finally I shall ask the same questions about God.

Realist, objective secular systems

The early Enlightenment reacted against the religious wars by looking for universal principles which could be justified independently of religious beliefs. Today ethicists summarize those principles as rights, duties and goals.

There are two kinds of rights. When you buy a bus ticket you have a right to ride on the bus. This right is the converse of somebody else's duty and is tied to a specific contract or law. We are concerned here, however, with natural rights (or human rights) which people claim to have over and above laws and contracts. There are three classic statements of natural rights. The first is the American Declaration of Independence (1776):

> We hold these truths to be self-evident, that all men are created equal, that they are endowed by their Creator with certain unalienable Rights, that among these are Life, Liberty and the pursuit of Happiness.[3]

The second is the French Revolution's Declaration of the Rights of Man and of the Citizen (1789):

> The aim of all political association is the preservation of the natural and imprescriptible rights of man. These rights are liberty, property, security, and resistance to oppression.[4]

The third is the United Nations Universal Declaration of Human Rights (1948):

> All human beings are born free and equal in dignity and rights. They are endowed with reason and conscience and should act towards one another in a spirit of brotherhood . . . Everyone has the right to life, liberty and security of person.[5]

Natural rights have no equivalent to the bus ticket. At first they were shorthand for describing moral rules given by God. Over time people came to think of them as self-evident things existing in their own right: just as the scientific laws of nature could exist independently of God, so they thought could natural rights.

Many people today still claim rights on this basis as though they are real things independent of human minds, like invisible shields in the sky giving moral protection to vulnerable people. If they are, the way to discover which rights exist will be to find the rights and 'read' them to see what they say. Of course we cannot do this. This is why talk of natural rights generates endless controversy: we have no method to find out, for example, whether the unborn baby has a right to live or the pregnant woman has a right to choose.

Even if these rights do exist, why should we respect them? As long as rights were a way of describing God's commands, whether we should honour them depended on what we believed about God; but once they are detached from God, and just float around handing out instructions, it is not clear why we should feel obliged to pay attention to them.

To illustrate the point, suppose one afternoon you are walking in a park with some friends, and you all notice an unusual cloud formation in the sky. The clouds perfectly form the words 'Do not eat potatoes'. Will you stop eating potatoes? Whether you do will probably depend on how you think those words got there. If you attribute the cloud formation to coincidence you will probably decide not to change your eating habits. If on the other hand you think the writing must be the work of clever minds with the necessary technology, you may speculate about who would have put the message there and what their motives are. Maybe everybody is being warned against a deadly disease. Or maybe someone has just got a grudge against potato farmers.

So also with natural rights. If they just happen to be there, as an odd fact about the universe, we have no reason to do what they tell us.

Many moral philosophers today defend natural rights, but not even the most realist of them seriously considers looking for them to discover what they say. Instead they try to develop accounts of rights which are internally consistent and justify credible moral commands. In other words, modern rights theorists have abandoned the idea of objective natural rights being 'out there' like shields in the sky waiting to be discovered. Instead they treat rights as a way of constructing a moral system. Natural rights have ended up as a social construct, not objective self-evident truths.

The same has happened to duties and goals. With duties the idea is that what exists objectively, over and above the human mind, is not rights but moral rules. The most influential defence of morality as duty is Immanuel Kant's *Critique of Practical Reason* (1788). According to Kant morality is a matter of transcending our desires and doing our duty.[6] His criterion for judging a rule to be a moral one is 'universalizability': a rule, a maxim, is moral if and only if 'I can also will that my maxim should become a universal law'.[7] Universalizability thus becomes *the* criterion of morality.

How do we know that universalizability is the supreme criterion for moral rules? Kant argued that it is one of those pieces of information built into the human mind. Few people would defend this today. Most people do have a moral sense, but it is not usually expressed as an obligation to do one's rational duty regardless of desire, nor as a principle of universalizability.

Even if this account of duty was built into all human minds, why should we obey it? Why not follow our desires rather than rationality? Kierkegaard responded to Kant by exploring this question.[8] Today, from an evolutionary perspective, it is all too easy to deny the authority of any idea just because it happens to be in all human minds.

Similarly with goals. The central figure of modern utilitarianism is Jeremy Bentham. Bentham believed the rational goal of human action is to maximize pleasure and minimize pain.[9] He proposed a classification of 12 pains and 14 pleasures which he thought should be able to test the happiness factor of any act.[10] Utilitarians today often speak of 'the greatest happiness for the greatest number'.

Bentham's great disciple John Stuart Mill recognized that our pains and pleasures cannot be measured against each other. Even if they could, nobody would know the right thing to do unless they calculated *all* the results of alternative courses of action, and we can never do that. Moreover, even if we could make all our decisions on the basis of maximizing pleasure and minimizing pain, we are still left with the question of why we should feel obliged to. Most people believe there is more to life than the pursuit of pleasure for its own sake.

Thus it turns out that all these realist accounts of morality have only survived by being turned into social constructs. In 1977 John Mackie proposed what he called an 'error theory' of ethics: 'Although most people in making moral judgements implicitly claim, among other things, to be pointing to something objectively prescriptive, these claims are all false.'[11]

Social constructs

Alternative theories of morality therefore describe it as something constructed by society. The idea of a social contract is that it is in everyone's interests to agree to live under a law and accept a government. The same can apply to morality: we all benefit if we can agree on a set of moral rules. Thus the seventeenth-century philosopher Thomas Hobbes argued that what is good is what anybody desires. If everyone tries to gratify their own desires without consideration of others, the result is a state of conflict in which few will have their desires gratified. So Hobbes saw morality, like laws, as a society's way to gratify as many desires as possible.[12]

Theories like this solve one problem but produce another. Wielenberg illustrates it with a story about an omnipotence contest. Whoever wins the contest is granted omnipotence. There are two competitors. The first plans to use his omnipotence for the good of humanity. He intends to bring peace, justice and happiness to the entire world. The second plans to slaughter most of humanity and force the rest to live in excrement pits, work themselves to death as his slaves and be tortured for his amusement. As it happens, the second competitor wins the contest and becomes omnipotent. It seems clear that the worst has happened – the world is on the verge of being plunged into evil. Fortunately, it does not happen. This is because when he becomes omnipotent the first thing he does is to change the moral rules. He makes it morally good to slaughter and torture, so that what he does turns out to be a life of supreme virtue. So all is for the best.

The point of the story is that we would not consider this a happy ending. We would want to say that even if he is omnipotent he cannot change the nature of good and evil by personal decree. This illustrates how we often judge the moral norms of our own society against a higher standard. Similarly, if you were living in Germany in the 1930s, and had a chance to betray a Jew in hiding from the authorities, you might think it would have been

> If you were living in Germany in the 1930s, and had a chance to betray a Jew in hiding from the authorities, you might think it would have been morally wrong to do so

morally wrong to do so. In other words we normally believe it is not just society that creates the moral rules; there is a higher moral authority which judges society's standards.[13]

If society creates the moral rules, why should any one individual assent to them? The rules may have been established mainly by the ruling classes, or more democratically, but in either case they have been created by human beings like you and me. Those people have the same kinds of minds and desires as you and I have, and it is not self-evident that you and I should obey the rules they create. Most people do accept most of the moral values of their own society, but it is common enough to dissent from some of them. This means that socially constructed morality only works to the extent that individuals choose to consent to it. If morality is a social construct, it depends on the consent of the individuals in that society. It seems that just as secular realist morality upon examination can be reduced to socially constructed morality, so also socially constructed morality can be reduced to individualistic morality.

Individually based morality

In individualistic systems, the authority which determines the moral rules is neither something superhuman, nor society, but each individual person. You are the highest authority on what is right and wrong for you.

A recent exponent of individualistic ethics was Philippa Foot. In 1959 she argued that we are given reasons for action when we are shown the way to something we want. We can divide our wants into two types. For some the question 'Why do you want that?' will make sense and a reason can be given. Thus, if we ask someone why he wants to live in a particular town, and he replies, 'Because I will not be lonely there', the question and answer make good sense; but the following question, 'Why do you not want to be lonely?', does not; not wanting to be lonely is just the way humans are. Moral judgements, when binding and universal, are based on achieving these basic wants.

Critics argued that this seems to invite us to live self-centred lives. In practice our moral views often conflict with what we want, and at other times what we want is at least partly influenced by our moral views. There was much discussion about the virtue of justice, which means being prepared to forego what we want.

Foot then changed her view. She still treated personal wants as the ground of morality, but included among them 'the sense of identification with others, that makes him care'. People have this tendency to care in varying degrees, and some do not have it at all. We cannot control our feelings, so there is no point telling people who lack this desire to care that they ought to have it. This means that moral judgements only apply to people who have the appropriate feelings.

On this basis Foot hoped people would see themselves as 'volunteers banded together to fight for liberty, etc.' and come into 'the moral cause'.[14] The difficulty with this is that an individualistic moral system can never provide a reason for doing so: if the highest moral authority is the individual, it is impossible to confront individuals with a moral appeal to something outside themselves. If rape and pillage is what I want to do, nobody has the moral authority to direct me otherwise.

Emotivism

If you are beginning to wonder whether morality means anything at all, you are not the first. In the early twentieth century logical positivists argued that all moral talk is meaningless.[15] They described moral language as emotivism. The classic analysis of emotivism was Charles Stevenson's *Ethics and Language* (1944). Stevenson argued that each moral statement is a combination of a factual statement with an imperative. 'This is wrong' means 'I disapprove of this; do so as well'. This leaves us wondering what is the point of talking about morality at all. After much linguistic analysis Stevenson comments: 'We seem forced to a distressingly meagre conclusion: if a man says "X is good", and if he can prove that he really approves of X, then he has all the proof that can be demanded of him.'[16] This raises the question of why we should pay any attention to other people's moral beliefs. Stevenson argued that all moral talk is really psychological manipulation.

This negative conclusion was foreseen by Nietzsche in the nineteenth century. Nietzsche argued that truth, justice, love, morality, religion and all human values and ideals are entirely the product of human invention and definition: 'all these values are, psychologically considered, the results of certain perspectives of utility, designed to maintain and increase human constructs of domination – and they have been falsely *projected* into the essence of things.' Originally expressions of the needs of life, they were turned into absolute values in themselves, and then turned against the needs of life. All morality, therefore, is an 'instinct of decadence', an 'instinct of denial of life'. As a result, 'now that the shabby origin of these values is becoming clear, the universe seems to have lost value, seems "meaningless".'[17]

Decline of secular authorities

To summarize so far: if moral truths really exist independently of the human mind, but not in a divine mind, there is no good reason why we should feel obliged to obey them. Upon examination all these moral authorities are really social constructs.

If moral truths are constructed by society, this means society's rules are morally right by definition. Few people really believe this. In addition, there is no compelling reason why any one individual should feel obliged to accept them. If you accept them, it is your personal decision. Socially constructed morality therefore turns out to be a consensus of the moral decisions of individuals.

If moral truths are constructed by individuals, each of us decides for ourselves what is to count as right and wrong for us, and for how long. Morality turns out to be nothing but individuals deciding what they want. To the extent that we try to impress our moral judgements on other people, we are engaging in psychological manipulation.

To simplify even further, we could focus on the question: what is the supreme moral authority? If human minds are the highest form of mind, then there is no authority above your mind to tell you what is right for you, nor any authority above the man with the gun, if he decides it would be a good idea to walk into a school and shoot at random.

Divine revelation

Moral philosophers debate how to rescue morality from the scrapheap. Because all these other theories upon examination can be reduced to some kind of error theory, perhaps we need to reconsider the God hypothesis.[18] The aim would be to explain morality in terms of a mind which has better access to the nature of reality than humans have. Such a mind would need to have moral intentions and be wise and benevolent. If there is such a being, we can ask my two questions of it.

First, how do we know what God's commands are? Ethicists have recently revived what they call 'divine command ethics'. In my view this is an unfortunate turn of phrase because it confuses two issues.

Fundamentalist Christian ethicists often argue that right and wrong, for Christians, is determined by the divine commands in the Bible. Secular ethicists often treat this view as characteristic of religious moral teaching, and reply that they do not need God to tell them the difference between right and wrong. Once again atheism speaks the same language as dogmatic religion, ignoring mainstream religious traditions.

> This approach ... means that Christian reasons for believing anything is right or wrong are completely different from secular reasons

I find this approach utterly unrealistic. It means that Christian reasons for believing anything is right or wrong are completely different from secular reasons. Some churches teach that this is indeed the case, but in practice Christians and non-Christians respond to murder, rape and global warming in the same kinds of ways.

I therefore prefer a natural law approach. We begin with life as we experience it, and we observe that some things make for a better life than others. This is to agree with social construct and individualist ethicists to the extent that individuals and societies work out from experience what are the good and bad things to do. We do not simply read off the moral rules, either from a set of natural rights or from the Bible. The difference only arises when we try to justify our moral judgements. If there is a higher moral authority than humans, it becomes possible to believe that this process of developing moral judgements is a matter of discovering moral truths, not merely inventing lifestyle choices.

God-based natural law can also take rights, duties and goals as guidelines which are useful most of the time. It differs from secular accounts of rights, duties and goals by being more flexible. One of the problems with the secular versions is that when one has decided which of the theories to adopt, one is faced with a list of principles or rules which then become *the* supreme moral authority. In practice, real life is too complicated. We could take any rule – the right to life, the rule not to steal, whatever – and somebody has been in a situation where we would agree that the rule ought to be broken in that case.

To turn to my second question: if we agree that morality is a matter of doing what God wants us to do, why should we obey God?

Ethicists often debate a passage in Plato's *Euthyphro*, where Socrates enquires about religious acts. Are they good things to do because the gods command them, or do the gods command them because they are good things to do? Secular ethicists find the story useful because it presents a case for separating morality from God. If good acts are only good because God commands them, God's commands are arbitrary and we have no reason to suppose that obeying God is a good thing to do. If on the other hand God commands them because they are good, then we ought to perform them because they are good, and the fact that God commands them becomes irrelevant. In either case we have no moral obligation to do something just because God commands it.

This argument presupposes its conclusion by assuming that the highest moral authorities are independent of God. In Plato's day people thought of the traditional gods as pretty immoral, so it made sense to think of moral norms as independent. This situation arose again in the Enlightenment when religious disagreement once more led to a search for explanations of morality independent of God. Today there are many Christians who believe the moral rules laid down by God cannot be rationally explained, so do appear to the human mind as arbitrary. Natural theology offers an alternative: that a morally good God created the universe with moral values in it, so that true moral values match the nature of the physical world. This means that moral truths are established by God, but are not arbitrary;

they are the way to achieve fulfilment and happiness in the world God has created.

Why should we obey God's moral rules? Because God has set up the universe so that better or worse outcomes are possible, depending on what humans choose to do, and has given us free will to choose between them. We are free to benefit ourselves at the expense of the common good, or to put the common good first.

I therefore believe that our two questions can only be satisfactorily answered by a God-based natural theology. It does however raise the question of why God would create human lives with this moral dimension and the potential to do evil as well as good. There is a characteristic religious answer, well expressed in the Bible. It is that God is a higher kind of being than humans, and invites us to share in that higher kind of being. To share it is to be holy. To be holy is only possible as a free choice. Characteristically holiness, and therefore moral goodness, is a matter of freely choosing the greater good, often at the expense of our own individual well-being.

To be a morally good person is therefore to direct our lives to the common good, with a more long-term hope of sharing God's holiness. The idea of sharing God's holiness does not itself tell us what we should or should not do, but it does provide the big picture, the objective towards which we rightly seek to move. Because decisions often have to be made quickly and with limited information we need guidelines, and societies work them out by reflecting on experience. We may sometimes describe these guidelines as rights, duties or the greatest happiness of the greatest number, but they are not absolute authorities in themselves. They are, rather, generalizations produced by the interaction of experience and our vision of holiness. There remains a need for personal judgement in each situation; we cannot simply read off from them exact commands telling us what to do, let alone telling us what other people ought to do. To make the best decisions, we can develop the practice of reflecting on what our lives are like, what they would be like if we realized our full potential, and how to make changes in the right direction. In this way, morality based on God is a morality of hope. It expects that life is full of potential, and that we really can make the world a better place.

I cannot prove that such a God exists, or that the universe has this character. It is a hypothesis. What I am proposing is that when we compare this answer with the answers we get when we apply the same questions to secular theories, the God hypothesis is the best way to make sense of morality. The only coherent alternative is that moral language is nothing but attempts to manipulate each other.

5

Religious experience

One of the most common reasons people give for believing in a greater being is a convincing inner experience. In this chapter I ask whether these experiences should be taken as evidence that there is such a being, or whether they are just a quirk of some people's brains. I begin with religious experiences in general, and at the end of the chapter turn to the distinctive features of out-of-the-body and near-death experiences.

To clarify the issue I begin with two descriptions. They are recorded in the Archive of the Alister Hardy Religious Experience Research Centre,[1] set up by Alister Hardy in 1969 and now at Lampeter University. It holds 6,000 accounts of religious experiences.[2]

1 My experience occurred when I was a child between ten and eleven years of age. Each day I was drawn to stand at a bedroom window at the back of our family terraced house in Pont-y-moel. I looked out between the sidewalls of the house across a narrow valley to the lower mountain levels of Mynydd Maen, which then rose steadily towards Twm Barlwm. For a year I was compelled to stand and wait and watch.

   On a day in March a column of luminous light appeared from one of the empty levels cut into the mountain which had been used for pigeon cots. It enclosed a figure, grew upwards and as it touched the clear blue sky disappeared, the waiting was over. I had no need to return to the window. I was not surprised at the 'appearance' but I was surprised that the intense need to go to the window had gone. This 'appearance' is as clear to me today as it was then, and I know that I experienced, in that moment, true reality. It is the single most important experience of my life.[3]

2 From out of nowhere, it seemed, I began asking myself 'Who am I?' I have no idea why I posed myself this question . . . I answered myself

with my first name – but immediately shook my head. The answer was preposterous, ridiculous! So obviously Not True! So I asked again 'Who am I?' and answered myself by saying 'woman'. That answer seemed almost equally absurd. I posed the question a third time and answered with the word 'human' this time. It felt as though I was having a conversation with a part of myself that was patiently sighing 'try again – you're just not getting it, are you?' So, once more I asked 'Who am I?' and this time I finally answered to my own satisfaction – 'I Am'. I suddenly felt as though I had shot through a telescope from one end to the other, from the microscopic end to the macroscopic end, and briefly experienced the world from the macroscopic end, whilst being aware that both exist simultaneously.

Since that time, I have read books on spirituality and human consciousness etc. and have come across the 'I Am' phrase to denote the 'Godly' or 'Divine' aspect of ourselves many times, but at the time of my own experience, I had had no prior knowledge or experience of this 'Am-ness' nor had come across those words in such a context.[4]

Stories like these are very common. Nobody takes all of them at face value. The question is: why take *any* of them at face value?

The standard starting point for research on religious experience is William James's *The Varieties of Religious Experience* (1902). James found that such experiences have four features:

1 Ineffability: they cannot be put into words.
2 Noetic quality: something has been learned.
3 Transiency: they do not last long.
4 Passivity: they seem to happen to the person rather than being something the person does.[5]

Later Alister Hardy collected people's spiritual or religious experiences, asking the question 'Have you ever been aware of or influenced by a presence or power, whether you call it God or not, which is different from your everyday self?'[6]

Since Hardy's time there has been a growing amount of research. Surveys indicate that between a third and a half of British people claim to have had direct personal awareness of 'a power or presence different from everyday life'. Much depends on exactly what question is asked, but the figure seems to be going up: a study by David Hay in 2001 found 76 per cent of the British population claimed awareness

Between a third and a half of British people claim to have had direct personal awareness of 'a power or presence different from everyday life'

of a transcendent reality.[7] Some believe the rise may reflect a change in culture: perhaps more people feel able to admit to spiritual experiences without thereby identifying themselves with belief systems they do not hold.[8] There has recently been large-scale research in China, India and Turkey. These countries were chosen because their cultural backgrounds are very different. Findings so far seem roughly similar, but because of language differences it is impossible to be certain that one is comparing like with like.[9] There is also a problem of people claiming to have religious experiences when they really mean something much more ordinary. The main groups are people with mental illnesses and members of religious groups which encourage people to think they have had a religious experience. Researchers need some criteria to distinguish the experiences they will count as authentic, and the main criterion is whether the experience has made a noticeable difference to the person's lifestyle.[10]

The term 'religious experience' implies that the experience reflects some kind of religious tradition. People who have these experiences often prefer to use the term 'spiritual experience' because it was nothing to do with any religion they know about. Researchers often use more neutral terms like 'transcendental experience', 'paranormal experience', 'peak experience' and 'mystical experience'.

They find four main types. The first is a distinctive way of experiencing aspects of the natural world, or the natural world as a whole. The second is a sense of presence – of God, an angelic being, or an ultimate supra-natural reality. The third is religious visions and auditions, both inner and outer. The fourth is a sense of unity with God or with the Ultimate, as reported by mystics.[11] They occur in all ages and cultures, and among religious and non-religious people alike.[12] Researchers have found that they are more prevalent among people with higher levels of education;[13] those who reject religious belief argue that this will be for evolutionary reasons.[14]

Researchers ask how subjects understand their experiences. Most, but not all, consider their experience life-enhancing, treasure it greatly and say it has led them to increasing concern for other people,[15] though a few report being frightened with a sense of the presence of evil.[16] Subjects say they cannot explain their experience merely in terms of the everyday world. They usually explain it with reference to some kind of higher power like a divine being.[17] Non-believers interpret their own experiences as part of the natural world but still consider them different in quality from ordinary experiences.[18] Believers and non-believers alike say their experience has revealed another dimension different from ordinary reality, or a deeper level of experience within reality,[19] and that this other dimension is more real than ordinary life.[20]

Granted that people have these experiences, do they provide evidence that there is a divine being? Any one experience on its own would only be weak evidence. The case is strengthened by three features: large numbers of people have them; they themselves are convinced that they have experienced another reality; and they lead to changes of lifestyle.

Sceptics argue that the experiences are just misinformation provided by the brain. This argument can take a stronger or a weaker form.

The stronger form is that religious experiences can be completely explained by brain processes. Epileptic seizures, surgical interventions in the brain and electrical stimulation of parts of the brain can all produce experiences of religious images and concepts. Such experiences, however, do not produce changes of lifestyle, nor do people afterwards look back on them as glimpses of a higher reality. Most religious traditions would not count them as authentic.[21] Nevertheless some people argue that because religious experiences can be correlated with stimulation of a particular part of the brain, therefore there is no truth in them. This is really a logical error. If you had the right wires attached to your brain a neuroscientist might be able to spot which part of your brain is being stimulated while you read this book. However clear the result was, the neuroscientist would not reach the conclusion that your perception of the book is completely explained by the brain processes. In addition, the book really is here. Similarly with religious experience: knowing which part of the brain is involved does not provide any evidence that your thoughts do not reflect reality.

The weaker form of the argument needs to be taken more seriously. This is that religious experience does not provide any knowledge, because of the way knowledge works. A religious experience may make you feel confident that there is a god, but you do not know it as certainly as we know that the earth goes round the sun and that antibiotics do not cure a cold.

Yet people who have the experience think they *do* know it as certainly. It is therefore worth clarifying the reason for judging that individuals' inner experiences do not count as knowledge. We have inherited a history of judgements on the matter. At the Reformation there was a movement called 'enthusiasm' which encouraged people to believe the Holy Spirit had given them direct knowledge. Unfortunately it also seemed that the Holy Spirit was telling different things to different people. The Enlightenment began partly as a reaction against this idea, arguing that knowledge claims can only be publicly accepted if the reasons for them are put into the public domain where others can examine them. In this way the Enlightenment produced two principles which have stood the test of time: all truth claims must be subjected to rational examination, and the rational examination must be public. All modern science is committed to these two principles.

However there is a catch. All public knowledge starts off as thoughts within an individual mind. If you measure a table and find it to be two metres long, the conclusion depends on remembering that you used the measuring tape correctly and used your eyes to read it. Behind all public knowledge lies an assumption that our inner subjective mental processes are normally reliable. We know we sometimes make mistakes, but we also know that unless we trust our mental processes we cannot know anything. Normally, the best stance to take with regard to our mental ideas is critical trust: in other words, we trust our experience except when we have reason to doubt it.[22]

The question therefore boils down to whether critical trust can be applied to religious experience. How does 'I had an inner experience and I know there is a god' differ from 'I am looking at this book so I know it exists'? There are three relevant differences.

First, sense experience is universal but religious experience only happens to some people.[23] This is true, but it is common in other situations too. We all depend on people who have skills and information that we do not have. Every time we use a telephone or switch on an electric kettle we are trusting that the designers of the machines have made accurate calculations which we do not know about.

Second, sense experience is largely uniform. If you show this book to your friends they will probably agree with you about what it looks like. When people have religious experiences they describe different divine beings.[24] If religious experiences express truths, why do they conflict with one another? Defenders of religious experience argue that it really does put people in touch with a divine being, but the divine being is not specific to any one religion. The research shows that people of all religions and none have such experiences.[25] Only 22 per cent of the people whose stories are recorded in the Hardy archive spontaneously use the word 'God' to describe the experience they have had. More often they claim that what they communicated with was 'ineffable', 'unknowable' or 'indescribable'.[26] John Hick has produced the best-known explanation. He distinguishes the transcendent as it is in itself from the way we think of it and experience it. In itself the transcendent is outside our concepts. Whatever concept we have of it is inadequate. There is an inbuilt human capacity to be aware that the transcendent is there, but the way we experience it is conditioned by our culture.[27]

Third, all our other information comes from the five senses. Religious experiences may make use of the five senses, but they seem to be generated by something different, a kind of sixth sense. How can we tell that this sixth sense is reliable?

This is a key question. We know that the world as we experience it is a minute fraction of the world known to science. We only hear a small part of the sound scale. We do not detect most of the chemicals in the environment. How then do we have any real knowledge at all? One extreme position is that we do not; the other extreme is that only the things we know about exist. Most thinkers take a moderate position, usually called critical realism; there is a real world out there, but our minds only notice some of what is going on. One analogy is that it is like catching things in a net. Our categories of thought form the mesh of our net. Only what can be caught in them is available to us and we fail to notice the rest.[28]

The claim is that religious experience catches elements of reality which our five senses miss.[29] This still leaves the question: how do we know that the bits it catches are true? Should we assume they are false unless we have corroboration from another source, or should we assume they are true unless we have reason to doubt them?

If we deny the value of these experiences because we already do not believe in God, we are begging the question. If we affirm them because we do believe, that too would beg the question. In order to answer the question fairly, we should put aside the answer we hope for and focus on the theoretical question. How do we normally expect to know things? If we take science as a guide we can argue that science is based on logic, mathematics and the evidence of the five senses. On the other hand, to insist that these are our only sources of information is to presuppose a positivist account of knowledge, as described in Chapter 1. Positivism fails to suffice because our knowledge also comes from imagination, instinct and intuition. In principle science works by beginning with human experience and trying to explain it. Rupert Sheldrake argues: 'To brush aside what people have actually

> 'To brush aside what people have actually experienced is not to be scientific, but unscientific'

experienced is not to be scientific, but unscientific. Science is founded on the empirical method, that is to say on experience and observation. Experiences and observations are the starting point for science, and it is unscientific to disregard or exclude them.'[30]

This is not to say that all religious experiences ought to be accepted as reliable insights; it only means they should not all be rejected as spurious. Each one should be judged on its merits.

Out-of-the-body and near-death experiences

I now turn to the distinctive features of out-of-the-body and near-death experiences. Out-of-the-body experiences usually take place during an operation. Afterwards the patient describes the experience of looking down on his or her body from above, as though hovering just below the ceiling, seeing and hearing what is going on but unable to communicate. It is this ability to describe what was going on which is most difficult to describe naturalistically, but it often happens.

A commonly cited case is that of Pam Reynolds. Pam is a professional musician who had a large operation to remove an aneurysm from her brain. To prevent blood circulating around her head during the operation her heart was stopped, her body temperature was lowered, and she was for all practical purposes temporarily dead with no measurable brain function. After the operation she could tell the doctors what had happened during it, to their astonishment. The interesting thing is that because Pam was a musician she was able to tell them that the drill which opened up her skull vibrated at a natural D. This drill had not been used until she was totally unconscious and none of the doctors had a clue about the musical note; but it turned out that she was right.[31]

Near-death experiences usually begin with an out-of-the-body experience. Typically, patients realize that they have died and then enter a dark tunnel with a bright, welcoming light at the end. There they seem to be met by a being of light and love, and often by their dead relatives as well. At this point they may get the message that their time is not yet ripe and they must return to their body, often against their will, and sometimes into pain. If they are not turned back at that point, they then experience a review of their life.

People who have near-death experiences often live completely transformed lives afterwards. Typical effects are greater compassion for other people and a more spiritual, less materialistic attitude to life. Many change to more caring professions, some become religious, and 82 per cent report that they no longer have any fear of death.[32]

> People who have near-death experiences often live completely transformed lives afterwards

Near-death experiences were first brought to public attention in 1975 with the publication of Raymond Moody's book *Life After Life*. In 1980 Kenneth Ring's *Life at Death* agreed with Moody's findings and described near-death experiences as occurring in five stages:

> peace (60 per cent); body separation (37 per cent); entering the darkness (23 per cent); seeing the light (16 per cent); entering the light (10 per cent).[33]

Religious experience

In 2001 the medical journal *The Lancet* published a study of near-death experiences, finding them to consist of the following elements: awareness of being dead (50 per cent); positive emotions (56 per cent); out-of-the-body experiences (24 per cent); moving through a tunnel (31 per cent); communication with the light (23 per cent); observation of colours (23 per cent); observation of celestial landscape (29 per cent); meeting with deceased persons (32 per cent); life review (13 per cent); presence of border (8 per cent).[34]

There are close similarities between these experiences and past religious teachings. The medieval Jewish text the *Zohar* says: 'We have learned that at the hour of a man's departure from the world, his father and relatives gather round him and he sees and recognizes them ... and they accompany his soul to the place where it is to abide.'[35] *The Tibetan Book of the Dead* states that when a person's 'consciousness-principle' gets outside its body 'he sees his relatives and friends gathered round weeping and watches as they remove the clothes from the body or take away the bed'. Researchers speculate that religious teachers had had, or knew of, near-death experiences.[36] Today with our advanced medical techniques they happen more often.

They do not suit everybody. A. J. Ayer (1910–89) was the first British philosopher to popularize logical positivism with his book *Language, Truth and Logic* (1936). In his distinguished career he argued that, far from God existing, the very idea of God has no meaning. In 1988, however, his heart stopped beating for four minutes. On resuscitation he told the doctor that he had seen a divine being and would have to revise all his previous books and opinions. This meant a complete reversal of everything he had stood for. A few weeks later he altered his account, saying, 'My recent experiences have slightly weakened my conviction that my genuine death, which is due fairly soon, will be the end of me, though I continue to hope it will.'[37]

Susan Blackmore, a leading researcher into near-death experiences, attributes them to naturalistic factors. She has had one such experience herself. She explains:

Severe stress, extreme fear and cerebral anoxia all cause cortical disinhibition and uncontrolled brain activity ... Tunnels and lights are frequently caused by disinhibition in the visual cortex, and similar noises occur during sleep paralysis ... Out of the Body experiences and life reviews can be induced by temporal lobe stimulation, and the positive emotions and lack of pain have been attributed to the action of endorphins and encephalins; endogenous opiates that are widely distributed in the limbic system and released under stress.[38]

Responding to the fact that many can describe what was happening to their own body, she attributes the descriptions to a combination of 'prior knowledge, fantasy, and lucky guesses and the remaining operating senses of hearing and touch'.[39]

The way to test this thesis is to find a control group of people with similar experiences and similar medical knowledge who have not had a near-death experience, and ask them to describe what they would have expected to see while they were being resuscitated. Penny Sartori did this with a study of heart attack patients in hospitals, published in 2006. About 25 per cent reported near-death experiences. Those who reported them were able to describe accurately the procedures undertaken during resuscitation, while those without them had no idea what had happened and were unable to guess correctly. (Sartori also placed pictures on the tops of cupboards in wards, in the hope that people might see them while they were out of their bodies, but nobody did.)[40]

> Those who reported them were able to describe accurately the procedures undertaken during resuscitation, while those without them had no idea what had happened and were unable to guess correctly

Conclusion

In general, the stories people give of their religious experiences seem to indicate a real, and common, communication with a transcendent being. However, it remains possible to interpret those experiences in ways which do not require the existence of such a being.

If they really do involve communication with a transcendent being, they affirm religious belief but have implications for believers. First, they do not distinguish between one religious tradition and another:

all are treated equally, as though all are partial expressions of a deeper reality, as Hick argues. This is particularly evident in the case of near-death experiences. Such evidence as there is makes no distinction between persons; apart from the life review, there is no indication that believers and unbelievers have different afterlives, still less that one religion is favoured above others. Religious traditions which claim to be the only true route to God are often, therefore, anxious to deny the validity of these experiences.

Second, we may ask why some people do not have them. Although some of the research findings indicate that most people have had at least one such experience in their lives, many say they have not. If there is a God, why does God not give everyone such an experience?

The best answer to this question is probably along the lines of diversities of personality. When researchers study religious experience they need to draw the line at experiences which cannot be decisively classified as such; but the experiences people have vary more widely. Religious believers relate to God in a variety of different ways: public worship, private prayer, meditation, caring for other people, moral commitment, appreciation of beauty, music, intellectual study. Nobody engages in depth with all these processes; some are drawn to one, some to another. To believe that not all of us are designed for deep inner experiences of the transcendent is consistent with believing that we are all designed to relate to God in some way or other. To take an example which would not fit the criteria of the researchers, music can generate feelings of a spiritual nature. It is easy to empathize with the sentiments of the Abba song 'Thank You for the Music', where the singer expresses gratitude for being able to give joy to others, but does not specify who is being thanked. This is a common experience: there are times when we feel grateful but do not know whom to thank. Similarly music can generate a sense of praise, and a sense that one is being transported into a different dimension of reality. As with the religious experiences described in this chapter, it is possible to believe that all we are really doing is enjoying ourselves in ways which for some obscure evolutionary reason the human brain happens to like; but once we have accepted that another dimension does exist, it makes better sense to explain the experiences as glimpses of it.

Nevertheless it remains possible to find explanations of the experiences which fit atheism. The key claim is that the mental processes involved are different from our normal ways of knowing things, and mislead us. However, we cannot know anything unless we presuppose that our mental processes are generally reliable. All our mental processes *sometimes* deceive us; what the unbeliever needs to claim is that this particular process *always* deceives. It turns out that once again the atheist position is being driven by a positivist account of knowledge, claiming that religious experience cannot provide true knowledge because it does not come from logic and the five senses.

In the case of values and morality, we found two coherent positions. The one which affirms God describes a rich world and immense potential for human life; the one which denies God describes an empty world and little potential for human life. In addition, atheists often try to recreate the richness of life and the world in the absence of God, but I have argued that the attempt fails. In the case of religious experience no such middle way is attempted; religious experiencers are simply encouraged to treat their experiences as a misleading trick of the mind. Tricks of the mind do happen – we all make mistakes – but in this case atheists invite us to believe that a particular type of experience *always* misleads. When we ask what leads them to the conclusion that it always misleads, the answer turns out to be a commitment to a positivist ideology.

In each of the last four chapters we have examined one of the common reasons for believing in God, and found that in each case the atheist alternative offers a bleaker account of reality. It empties the world of dimensions which give our lives their significance. Atheism cannot be disproved; but if we find that our experience of life cannot be squeezed into that empty world, it makes better sense to believe in God.

In the course of these examinations we have come across other reasons for belief which are less common, but still make a contribution. We shall explore them in the next three chapters.

6

Necessary being

———◆·●·◆———

One of the joys of living in my part of Liverpool is that I often catch a bus from the Holy Land to Paradise Street. Recently a neighbour asked me how to make the journey. I advised her to go to the stop on Park Road and catch an 82 bus. Such an ordinary, everyday conversation does not, on the face of it, require any complex theories, but in fact it makes a wide range of presuppositions. Before asking, the neighbour probably did not wonder about the chances that Paradise Street had been destroyed by an earthquake the previous night, or whether she was actually a brain in a vat fantasizing about my existence. Similarly, when I answered I presupposed that I was not a brain in a vat, that my neighbour was a human being with thoughts and intentions comparable to mine and capable of reading bus numbers, and that the buses were still running. We did not prove any of these presuppositions, and if we had tried she would not have got her shopping done.

Even the simplest of communications make a huge range of presuppositions. If we decided to make a list of our presuppositions we would not spot all of them. When discussing belief in God, therefore, we need to ask not only whether it makes better sense of our conscious beliefs but also whether it makes better sense of our presuppositions. This chapter and the next two relate belief in God to some essential presuppositions.

When early Enlightenment philosophers set out to show how reason could establish the existence of God, they produced a range of arguments, three of which are still debated by philosophers of religion.

The design argument was discussed in Chapter 2; the other two, the ontological and cosmological arguments, will be the topic of this chapter. As they have much in common it will be helpful to consider them together. 'Ontological' means about being and 'cosmological' means about the universe.

Ontological argument

The ontological argument is usually dated from Anselm, Archbishop of Canterbury in the eleventh century. The revival of learning in western Europe was just beginning. At the time nobody doubted that God existed; the question was whether logic could prove it.

The simpler version of the argument is rarely defended today. Anselm defined God as 'a being than which no greater can be conceived'. By 'greater' he meant something like more perfect.[1] Referring to a text in a psalm which says 'The fool has said there is no God',[2] he replied that even the fool does in fact conceive of a being than which no greater can be conceived. He proceeded to argue that if such a being did not exist, we would be able to conceive of a greater being, namely one such which did exist. The greatest conceivable being must therefore have existence.

Descartes, writing six centuries later at the beginning of the Enlightenment, defended the argument using the analogy of a triangle. He could imagine a triangle that did not exist, but even this imaginary triangle must have certain properties, like having angles that add up to 180 degrees. Just as having such angles is implied in the very idea of a triangle, so existence is implied in the very idea of God.[3] Two centuries later again Immanuel Kant objected that to say God possesses the property of existence is to presuppose that there is a God.

Modern defenders of the ontological argument[4] usually focus on Anselm's second account, which distinguishes between necessary and contingent existence. This distinction is relevant to the cosmological argument as well. Something exists contingently when it just happens to exist but might not have. Contingent things can exist at one time but not another. Something which exists necessarily must always exist. Philosophers today debate what might exist necessarily; apart from

God, some of the other candidates are numbers, space, time and the rules of logic.

The argument is that if there is something so great that nothing greater can be conceived, it would have to exist necessarily. This is because by definition anything which exists necessarily cannot come into existence and go out of existence. It cannot be caused by something else, so it must depend on itself alone. Therefore either it never exists or it always exists. Some defenders of the argument point out that therefore the existence of God is either necessary or impossible – one or the other – but since we cannot prove it impossible the only other alternative is that God necessarily exists.[5]

Many people find the ontological argument unconvincing because it seems to claim that pure logic can make something exist. John Hick writes: 'Logical necessity has no purchase on matters of fact and existence . . . It cannot be logically necessary that there is a reality corresponding to the concept of an ontologically necessary being – or indeed to any other concept.'[6] Keith Ward replies that the argument is not using words to bring something into existence: it is analysing the way we understand reality, and concluding that if the way we understand reality has any truth in it, we have to presuppose a necessary being. If we accept this, then we can bring other considerations into play to ask whether this necessary being would have to be something like God.[7]

The ontological argument continues to generate extreme reactions. For some it is too absurd to be worth bothering with. Others say it is a deep insight into the nature of reality and once they have grasped it they cannot deny it.

I doubt whether anyone has ever come to faith in God as a result of it. For Anselm, there was no serious doubt about the existence of God: what he was exploring was the power of reason. Descartes, at the beginning of the Enlightenment, still took for granted the existence of God, but used the ontological argument as part of his case for showing that reason can produce knowledge independently of the dogmas of church leaders. By the time of Kant the presuppositions had been reversed. He could take for granted the authority of human reason, but treat the existence of God as subject to reasoned examination of the evidence, just like everything else. It is this way round that the argument gets debated today.

Cosmological argument

The cosmological argument is usually dated from the ancient Greek philosopher Plato. Plato proposed that, because everything that moves is moved by something else, there must have been a first mover. The only kind of reality that can produce spontaneous movement is soul.[8] Putting it into today's language, we might say that if you have a mind with free will you may decide to do something, but if you do not you are part of a determined sequence of causes and effects. Plato thought there must have been a mind which got things moving in the first place. His pupil Aristotle agreed, arguing that otherwise there would have to be an infinite regress of movers.[9]

This argument was picked up in the thirteenth century by Thomas Aquinas. Of Aquinas' 'five ways' of reasoning towards the existence of God, his fourth and fifth are roughly the moral argument and the design argument; the first three are relevant here. The first restates Plato's argument to an unmoved mover. The second appeals to causation: 'In the observable world causes derive their causality from other causes; we never observe, nor ever could, something causing itself, for this would mean it preceded itself ... So one is forced to suppose some first cause, to which everyone gives the name *God*.[10]

If we treat these two arguments together, the question is: is there an infinite regress of causes, or was there a first cause, a first mover? A first cause would have to be uncaused, so somehow self-explanatory, and we are back to the idea of a necessary being.

Today there is an alternative. Some theoretical physicists believe that time does not always go from the past to the future, but somehow curves in on itself so that there was no beginning. If we accept this theory, then we no longer need to choose between an infinite historical regress and an original self-explanatory first cause.

> Some theoretical physicists believe that time ... somehow curves in on itself so that there was no beginning

Aquinas of course did not know about this more recent theory, but he did allow for something similar. In his day there was disagreement about whether the universe had existed from eternity as Aristotle had taught, or had been created at a point in time as Christianity taught. To allow for either possibility he distinguished two kinds of causation. When you got up this morning you may have switched a light on. It may still be on. This is a historical sequence: first the cause, then the effect. If you are having a hot bath, and your skin feels hot and wet, the cause of the hot and wet feeling does not precede the effect; both are taking place at the same time. Aquinas described the first cause as the top of a hierarchical sequence, continually making the universe work, not the start of a historical sequence. Later Newton's account of momentum made this hierarchical sequence seem unnecessary, but it seems to fit rather well the theory of time curving in on itself. This is because, although it dispenses with the need for either an infinite historical regress of causes or an original self-explanatory cause at the beginning, it raises instead the question of why there is something rather than nothing. In this case, although we are no longer looking for a historical sequence, we are still looking for a cause, and we are still faced with the same two options: either there must be an infinite sequence of causes, or there must be an original self-explanatory cause, a starter motor as well as a battery, an unmoved mover.

Aquinas' 'third way' is specifically about the distinction between contingent and necessary existence. If everything was contingent, coming into and out of existence, with each thing caused by some other contingent thing in an infinite regress, over an infinite time every possibility would be realized. This would include the state at which nothing existed. However, if there was ever a time when nothing existed, it would have been impossible for anything to come into existence. There must therefore be a being which exists not contingently, but necessarily.[11]

As it stands this argument is unsatisfactory. There could be an infinite time without every possible state realized: there may for example be a limited set of states which keep recurring.[12]

An alternative version is easier to defend. The universe has been full of contingent things ever since the Big Bang. If the Big Bang was a contingent event, was it caused by another contingent event, or by something necessary? What matters most to us is the laws of nature. We depend on them carrying on as they are. Physicists now believe the laws of nature were established in the first fraction of a second after the Big Bang. If the Big Bang was a contingent event caused by another contingent event, then the laws of nature are also contingent. Far from being universal and unbreakable, they came into existence at a particular time and place, accidentally, for no known reason, and therefore we have no way of knowing how long they will last. They seem to have lasted well for fourteen billion years, but for all we know our lives may depend on fourteen billion of them and any one of them could give up tomorrow. If the whole of reality is just an accident, the laws of nature *could* be reliable, just by luck, but we have no way of knowing. Perhaps as you walk down the street tomorrow morning gravity will stop working and you will float into the sky. We assume it will not happen, but we make this assumption because we put more trust in the laws of nature than we can justify. We treat them as reliable and eternal – that is, we treat them like gods – while physicists tell us that on the contrary they are contingent and limited.

> If the Big Bang was a contingent event, was it caused by another contingent event, or by something necessary?

Experience tells us that we have to live our lives as though the universe is ordered and reliable. Pragmatically, we have no choice but to assume that it is; but can we justify the assumption? In order to do so, we need to believe that the universe is not entirely contingent. Such a belief is just a vague hope, unless we can produce a credible theory to explain what there is behind all the contingent events to establish order and reliability. There would have to be something which is not accidental or temporary: in other words a necessary being.

This version of the cosmological argument offers a theory of reality to justify the trust we place in the laws of nature. It would mean that all the contingent events we know about, including the laws of nature, have their origin in something which is not chance, not accident, not here today and gone tomorrow, because it exists necessarily.

This is speculation, of course. It may not be the case. What it shows, however, is that if it is not the case – if there is no such necessary being – then not only do we have no reason to believe in God, but we have no reason to believe in science either. We cannot expect science to produce reliable knowledge unless there is some kind of reliable necessary being giving the universe its coherence. Once again, it seems that either science works and religion works, or neither.

Conclusion

The arguments I have described in this chapter are not the usual reasons why people do or do not believe in God. What they claim is that if science can really do what we normally think it does, it needs to make certain presuppositions. One is that there needs to be a necessary being something like what we mean by God. Of course we may be exaggerating the powers of science: some non-realists think we are in a chaotic, accident-prone universe and the appearance of order is just a trick of the human mind. (Or, more precisely, a trick of *your* mind, since on this hypothesis you have no way of knowing whether anybody else has a mind; your neighbours may be robots.) Moreover, even if our ability to make sense of the world depends on presupposing a necessary being which is the ultimate cause of the universe, we are a long way from identifying that cause with the kind of God that religious believers believe in. What believers then do is explore additional reasons for describing the necessary being in greater detail.

For a few centuries church leaders had power to restrict the advance of science. Scientists defended themselves by drawing a line to separate science from religion. As a result modern western science still expects to operate without any reference to God. This taboo on God is now hindering the advance of science. Historically, it went along with a similar taboo on all unobservables. Scientists have long since abandoned the taboo on unobservables. If they could now let go of the taboo and treat God as a possible explanatory hypothesis – along with black holes, string theory, the square root of minus one and countless other unobservables – it would once again become possible to have an integrated account of reality in which scientists and theologians could work together on explaining the universe.

None of this proves that there is a God. It remains a hypothesis. Like all scientific hypotheses, if it is the best one we have got the normal procedure would be to accept it until such time as we can improve on it.

Necessary being

The arguments in favour of a necessary being, ontological and cosmological, appeal to a fundamental nature of reality which science needs to presuppose. It is not the only presupposition scientists need to make. Two others are that the world is ordered and that the human mind can understand its order. These will be the topics of the next two chapters.

7

Order

This chapter and the next are about knowledge, with a focus on science. Atheists often argue that science offers a sufficient account of reality and makes God superfluous. My aim here is to show that this is something science cannot do, however much information it provides. I shall do this by describing two presuppositions on which all science depends. These presuppositions now seem common sense. They are so much part of our mental furniture, at least in modern western society, that we take them for granted as self-evident. In fact theologians debated them for thousands of years; they only came to seem reliable truths because certain beliefs about God came to dominate, and it was only then that modern science was able to develop.

These two presuppositions are that the world is ordered and that the human mind can understand its order. If we did not take them for granted most of our knowledge would be undermined. Science cannot prove either of them because it has to take them on trust before it can do anything at all.

They have a similar history. It was in the high Middle Ages that European intellectuals broadly accepted them. The main reason was the convergence of thought between Jews, Christians and Muslims who all believed the world had been created by a single powerful and good God, and that God had deliberately created an ordered world and given us minds capable of understanding it.

Once these presuppositions were established they made modern science possible. By the end of the seventeenth century most educated Europeans believed that human reason must be reliable because a good God would not deceive us.

A century later the roles had been reversed. It was reason which was absolutely reliable, while God existed if and only if reason could prove it. Hence the famous comment the French scientist Laplace is reputed to have made, when Napoleon asked why he had not mentioned God in his theory: 'No, Sire, I had no need of that hypothesis.'

Today science normally proceeds without referring to God. It is possible to think that belief in a God of order was just a historical step on the way to establishing modern science. On the other hand perhaps these two presuppositions, order and intelligibility, cannot be justified in any other way. I shall examine the two presuppositions respectively in this chapter and the next, and ask the question: when scientists keep God out of the picture, are they sawing off the branch they are sitting on?

> It is possible to think that belief in a God of order was just a historical step on the way to establishing modern science

If they are sawing it off, we would expect the prestige of science to decline in places like the UK where God is not treated as essential to understanding reality. Many scientists believe it is indeed declining. Writers like Ben Goldacre repeatedly complain that the mass media distort serious scientific research in the interests of popular sensationalism, because most newspaper proprietors find sales improve this way.[1] Recent government changes to university funding have nearly always been in the direction of taking money away from pure research and replacing it with projects funded by particular vested interests. Since the 1960s there has been a rapid increase in the practice of witchcraft and associated magical activities. These may all be disconnected temporary fashions, but there are also intellectuals arguing that the world is not ordered or that the human mind cannot understand it.

If we did not presuppose order, we would not have a clue what will happen next. We put roofs on the tops of our houses because rain always comes down from above; but if the world is not ordered, maybe it will come upwards through the floor next time. Such an idea seems absurd. We discount it because we presuppose that the world functions according to ordered regularities. All science, and most of our other knowledge, would be impossible otherwise.

It is not self-evident. We observe some regularities, like the alternation between day and night, but also some irregularities like the weather and other people's behaviour. It is possible to believe that the world is basically ordered and seek explanations for the irregularities, but it is also possible to believe that the world is basically chaotic and seek explanations for the regularities.

Premodern theories

Today we are so used to taking order for granted that it is difficult to imagine what life would feel like if we did not. Here are two ancient texts which describe the world differently. The first is a story from Homer's *Iliad*. During the Trojan war, the hero Achilles kills a lot of Trojans in the River Scamander. The river speaks: 'If the Son of Cronos [the god Zeus] really means you to kill all the Trojans, I implore you at least to drive them away from me and do your foul work on the plain. My lovely channels are full of dead men's bodies . . .' After some more speeches,

> The great spearman Achilles leapt from the bank and plunged into the middle of the stream. Scamander rushed on him in spate. He filled all his channels with foaming cataracts, and roaring like a bull he flung up on dry land the innumerable bodies of Achilles' victims that had choked him, protecting the survivors by hiding them in the deep and ample pools that beautified his course. The angry waters rose and seethed around Achilles; they beat down on his shield and overwhelmed him.[2]

This is an epic about an age of heroes in the distant past. It echoes an ancient belief that natural phenomena like rivers had minds of their own, spirits. Suppose we really believed that every time a river floods or dries up, it is because the river itself has decided to do so for its own reasons? If we start thinking about the practical implications, they are immense. For example, it would be foolish to build a reservoir unless the river could be persuaded to accept it. Similarly, computer-owners often say their computer has a mind of its own; but if it really did, it would be no use at all.

The following is an ancient Mesopotamian prophecy. The god Adad is speaking through a prophet, warning the king to do his duty and burn the expected sacrifices:

In oracles has Adad, lord of Kallassu, spoken thus: 'Am I not Adad, lord of Kallassu, who have brought him upon my knee and set him upon the throne of his father's line? After I set him upon his father's throne, I have also given him a dwelling. Now, as I have set him upon the throne, so I can take Nihlatu out of his hand. If he does not fulfil the provision I am lord over the throne, the district and the city, and I can take from him what I have given him. But if he fulfils my desire, I shall give him thrones upon thrones, houses upon houses, districts upon districts, cities upon cities, and I shall give him the land from the west to the east.[3]

This time the emphasis is on the king's success in government and war. Suppose we were all to believe that the future of our society depended on whether the government was good at appeasing the gods with the proper sacrifices? Again, the difference would be immense.

Ancient myths about gods were not just fictions. They normally had their origins in attempts to explain things. Often they began from issues of security. Today when disaster threatens we try to work out what is causing it so as to prevent it: anxiety about global warming and terrorism, for example, motivates governments to work out how to respond. In the same way the ancients responded to floods, plagues and military defeat by asking what caused them and what to do about them. The main difference is that be-cause they believed major disasters were caused by gods, their solutions usually meant burning sacrifices; otherwise they were, like us, trying

> In a world where any known regularities could be contravened without warning by gods with their own agendas, science as we know it was impossible

to explain why disaster happened in order to make sure it did not happen again. In a world where any known regularities could be contravened without warning by gods with their own agendas, science as we know it was impossible.

Out of all the ancient religions, the one practised by the tiny state of Judea became the basis for three of the world's major religions today, and provided a basis for science to develop. Most of the other religions have died out altogether. What was different about the Judeans?

Normally, history is written by the winners. It is the winners who impose their values and their theories of reality on the losers. Just occasionally this does not happen. When Judea was defeated by the Babylonians and its people taken into exile in the sixth century BCE, usual practice would have been to abandon worship of their god – who had failed to protect them – and transfer allegiance to Marduk, the god of the Babylonians. However, about 50 years later the Persians attacked Babylon. Cyrus, the Persian leader, had a policy of allowing exiles to return home. An anonymous poet, usually called Second Isaiah, interpreted his victory as part of an international plan by Israel's god. Normally gods of small nations were not expected to have international plans, but the poet identified Israel's god with the supreme God of the whole world. For once, the beliefs of the losers were vindicated.

> The poet identified Israel's god with the supreme God of the whole world. For once, the beliefs of the losers were vindicated

Losers and winners usually have different moral values and theories of reality. The dominant values are established by the winners. The losers often accept them; losers can only convincingly reject the dominant values when they can also offer an alternative account of reality complete with an alternative account of what needs to be done.

Most ancient near eastern creation stories explained how the gods related to each other and why they created the world. Typically the world was made by a young god who was stronger than the older gods and gave the ruling classes authority to govern. This meant the world was ordered, but contingently. It might change if the supreme god changed his mind or was overthrown by other gods. Each time one empire overthrew another, the change could be described in terms of one god becoming more powerful than another. The new world order would be based on what the new god wanted. In this world-view it was possible to believe that how crops grow, how diseases spread and how babies are born were all in principle up for review when a new god took over. The order of nature was therefore relative, and often threatened. To keep human society viable depended on the expertise of the ruling classes with their knowledge of how to please the gods. Similarly today, when governments debate how to save the nation from economic disaster, their theoretical analyses are different but fundamentally they are doing the same kind of thing: using elite expertise to manipulate the conditions of human life in the general interest as they conceive it.

The Judeans had a loser's perspective. They refused to accept that the world order depended on the ruling classes with their expertise. When they edited their scriptures they prefaced them with a statement of the order they did believe in.

Unfortunately, the first chapter of Genesis needs decontaminating before we can appreciate what the authors were claiming. The text does say that the world was made in six days complete with every species of living being, but this was background information taken for granted in those days; there are similar statements in other ancient near eastern creation stories. What the authors of Genesis were positively claiming, contrary to the other stories of their time and place, was that the world had been created by a different kind of god and therefore had a different nature. It was that difference which would, in time, make modern science possible.

> What the authors of Genesis were positively claiming was that the world had been created by a different kind of god and therefore had a different nature

> In the beginning when God created the heavens and the earth, the earth was a formless void and darkness covered the face of the deep, while a wind from God swept over the face of the waters.   (Genesis 1.1–2)

In Genesis the world order has been intentionally designed, by the only God. There are no threats from competing gods. Nor is there any favour towards the ruling classes. Instead there is a repeated refrain: each time God performs an act of creation, God looks at it and declares it good.

The fundamental order of the universe is established in the first three acts of creation, each one a separation:

> Then God said, 'Let there be light'; and there was light. And God saw that the light was good; and God separated the light from the darkness. God called the light Day, and the darkness he called Night. And there was evening and there was morning, the first day.   (Genesis 1.3–5)

Hebrew scholars see this alternation of day and night as a way of saying God created time. There is an inconsistency: later on the text describes God creating the sun and the moon, even though they knew that light comes from the sun. We know the reason. One thing we owe to the ancient Babylonians is astrology: the Babylonians believed that the heavenly bodies were gods who could see and influence events on earth. Genesis suppresses the idea. The creation of time comes first, expressed through the alternation of day and night, while the sun and moon are emphatically demoted.

The second separation is the vertical one:

> God said, 'Let there be a dome in the midst of the waters, and let it separate the waters from the waters.' So God made the dome and separated the waters that were under the dome from the waters that were above the dome. And it was so. God called the dome Sky. And there was evening and there was morning, the second day. (Genesis 1.6–8)

Throughout the ancient near east it was taken for granted that the earth is flat and the sky above it is a solid inverted bowl. English translations of the Bible sometimes translate it as 'firmament', sometimes as 'dome'. It is the blue thing we see when we look up at the sky on a sunny day. The Hebrew word literally means something that has been hammered out; Homer described it as made of iron. Of course this is not at all our understanding of the sky. Genesis again accepts the science of its day, while turning it into a claim that the vertical dimension of space has been established by God from the beginning.

The third separation is the horizontal one:

> And God said, 'Let the waters under the sky be gathered together into one place, and let the dry land appear.' And it was so. God called the dry land Earth, and the waters that were gathered together he called Seas. And God saw that it was good. (Genesis 1.9–10)

In these three acts of separation God establishes time, and the vertical and horizontal dimensions of space. Other creation stories had their own accounts of which god created the world, and how; what makes the Judean one distinct is their conviction that there is only one god. This text therefore exudes a confidence that God's plans will never be undermined. The order God has created is permanent. Thus the Jews, deprived of their own king and empire, came to believe in a universal God-given order which remains the same independently of the ups and downs of military power.

This commitment to a single God of order, though very much the driving force behind the Old Testament as we have it now, was not universally accepted thereafter. Jews and Christians have often adopted contrasting beliefs. In the Middle Ages most Europeans believed the world around them was more chaotic, full of unpredictable angels and demons. This was not true of the educated classes, who were less inclined to attribute real power to them, and by the end of the seventeenth century their view had come to prevail. The historian Keith Thomas, discussing the role of magic in the witch hunts, writes:

> Apart from the influence of individual miscarriages of justice, it is possible to discern the growth of two essentially novel attitudes. The first is the assumption of an orderly, regular universe, unlikely to be upset by the capricious intervention of God or Devil. This view of the world was consolidated by the new mechanical philosophy, but the way to its acceptance had long been prepared by the emphasis of theologians upon the orderly way in which God conducted his affairs, working through natural causes accessible to human investigation.[4]

Bases of modern science

Medieval scholars debated how free God is in running the world. At one extreme, Neoplatonists believed the world had emanated from God through a determined process of the lesser emanating from the greater, so that everything that happens is determined and could not have been otherwise. On this account the world's order is unintended and unlimited: unintended because God had no choice, and unlimited because nothing lies outside the determined sequence of cause and effect. Except for the limitation of human freedom, to which we shall return in the next chapter, such a reliable order made science plausible. At the other extreme, some theologians argued that God is completely free, and therefore under no obligation to do anything regularly. From this it followed that we cannot know what God will do tomorrow, so science cannot work.

The order expressed in Genesis is between the two extremes. Order implies regularity, but regularity is intended and limited. Because it is intended, by God, we can ask *why* the laws of nature are the way they are, and expect the answers to lie in God's intentions. Because regularity is limited, it is possible to believe that some things, most importantly the human mind, lie outside the sequence of determined cause and effect. The way the medievals expressed this view was to distinguish between God's absolute power and God's regular power: in principle God can do anything possible, but in practice God does what is good for creation; and that means maintaining order.

Gradually God's regular power, the things God does in an ordered way, came to be known as the laws of nature. According to the seventeenth-century researcher Helmont, God determined the properties of things at their creation; what we call 'nature' is just the effect of that decree: 'I believe that Nature is the command of God, whereby a thing is that which it is, and doth that which it is commanded to do or act . . . For that most glorious Mover hath given powers to things, whereby they of themselves and by an absolute force may move themselves or other things.'[5]

The two leading scientists of the later seventeenth century disagreed about how God made this happen. To Leibniz, when God created the universe he made it intrinsic to each thing to do what it does, thus investing matter with an energy which would continue indefinitely: 'The same force and vigour remains always in the world, and only passes from one part of matter to another, agreeably to the laws of nature, and the beautiful pre-established order . . . Whoever thinks otherwise, must needs have a very mean notion of the wisdom and power of God.'[6] Leibniz was concerned to establish that God got creation right first time; any subsequent need to tinker with it would show that it was badly made. Newton, on the other hand, argued that this would make God completely irrelevant, except as the original creator. According to Newton, God was needed not only as the original creator, but also to push the planets back into their correct orbit from time to time. Each accused the other of not giving enough credit to God.

Order without God

Thereafter, as the commitment to the centrality of God gradually declined, the laws of nature came to be seen as self-explanatory. Many people today think they are. However, this overlooks two gaps in the account, both of which already troubled David Hume in the eighteenth century.

One is causation. When we say that one event causes another, our evidence is that the second repeatedly follows the first. Sometimes a particular combination of events is coincidence, but then we have no reason to make predictions based on it. Science is only possible when we interpret regular combinations of events in terms of cause and effect. Hume pointed out that what we observe is only the repeated patterns of events; it is our minds which supply the idea that the first *causes* the second. Nevertheless, our observations provide no justification for this idea.[7]

To take an example, one of the laws of nature is that water boils at 100° C under normal atmospheric pressure. If you put a pan of water on the cooker, stick a thermometer in it and turn on the gas, when it gets to 100° C you will see bubbles. What you will not see is a bubble-making machine. We know your water will boil at 100° C because that is how water always behaves. The normal scientific explanation is in terms of the additional energy affecting the molecular bonds. Thus scientific explanations tell us what happens in ever greater detail, drawing attention to the regularities, but they do not tell us what makes it happen. This inability of science to explain how causes cause their effects is well known. What is less well known is that it is a direct result of banishing God. We have seen how Leibniz and Newton agreed that God makes each effect follow its cause, while disagreeing about how God does it; Hume, omitting God altogether, could see that causation could no longer be explained.

What is missing from the explanation is some kind of force. It is easy to overlook the problem because the word 'law' usually implies some kind of force, like a police force. We may then imagine that 'laws of nature' are forces. Physicists often use words like 'force', 'momentum' and 'gravity' as though they were indeed real powers; after all, it would be impossible to study nature without presupposing that causes *somehow* cause their effects.

The dilemma, then, is that once God is taken out of the picture, the laws of nature are very good at telling us what happens, but give us no inkling about what kind of force makes it happen. For most people this does not matter; we can shrug our shoulders and accept that nobody knows why water boils at 100° C, while feeling confident that our eggs will cook in the future as they always have done. Some pragmatist scientists adopt this position, arguing that science should be judged purely on its results and should abandon any attempt at real truths about the way the universe works.

> Once God is taken out of the picture, the laws of nature are very good at telling us what happens, but give us no inkling about what kind of force makes it happen

For most scientists, however, looking for explanations of reality is the primary task of science; to abandon this search is to abandon science. Some therefore argue that in order to explain how the laws of nature make things happen there must be real forces, even though science cannot tell us what they are. We can go further: given the way causation works, we can make some observations about what these forces must be like. They would have to be reliable, invisible, powerful forces with the ability to make things happen regularly the way they do. We need go no further: it is clear where we are heading. The ancients and medievals believed in forces like these, and called them gods.

Related to causation is the problem of induction. Science proceeds by observing that one thing follows another with regularity, analysing the regularity as a law of nature, and then predicting that the same regularity will also take place on occasions which we have not observed. Because the sun has always risen in the east, we assume it will rise in the east tomorrow. Hume acknowledged that this principle of induction is essential to science, but puzzled over the fact that there was no good reason to suppose it to be true, or even probable.[8]

Since Hume's time the significance of this problem has increased considerably. Until the beginning of the twentieth century it seemed that the whole of reality was contained within a single universe of fixed size, the wide range of things in it all consisted of nothing but atoms, and every atom behaved according to the universal and eternal laws of nature described by Newtonian physics. Many believed science would in time establish a complete account of how the universe works. Today it seems the universe is ever-expanding and for all we know may be one of countless billion universes. Atoms, far from being the bedrock, indivisible substance composing all things, have been split and ever-smaller parts are being studied. More unnerving still is the demotion of Newtonian physics. Taken for granted for two centuries as the truth about how the whole universe works and always will work, the theory is now understood to explain only a limited range of events in it. Furthermore, not a single scientific law is guaranteed exemption from the same fate; any of our theories about the universe may eventually turn out to be true only of the bit we can see now. To add to the uncertainties, even if all our known laws of nature are indeed accurate, the more of them we discover the more we find greater complexities still beyond our understanding. The overall result is that, although we know a lot more than we did a century ago, we are far more aware that our knowledge only covers a tiny proportion of the universe's processes, and even what we do know is only provisional.

Given these limitations it is hardly surprising that increasing numbers of people have been asking whether our science is true at all. Perhaps the order and regularity we seem to see is just a figment of our imagination, our way of interpreting chaos as if it were ordered.

> Perhaps the order and regularity we seem to see is just a figment of our imagination

This is what non-realists often argue. Two hundred years ago Immanuel Kant made a distinction between things as they are in themselves and things as they appear to us. Realists believe that outside our minds there is a big wide world, and it would still be there if we did not exist. Non-realists point out that we can never know whether our ideas of reality represent reality itself. We have no way of independently getting outside our minds to check whether we are getting it right. Reality-for-us is the only reality we shall ever know.

The most influential critique of realist science has been Thomas Kuhn's *The Structure of Scientific Revolutions* (1962). According to Kuhn, most scientific research works within the dominant theoretical framework of the time and accepts its methods. From time to time the framework gets stuck with insoluble problems, a revolution takes place and a new framework takes over. Kuhn argued that, because method depends on theory, different frameworks have different methods. If the difference is big enough it becomes impossible to agree how to describe the results of experiments or what would be a rational method to resolve disagreement. There is then no objective basis on which to judge which is the better framework. Kuhn argued that over the long term there is therefore no gradual progress from inferior scientific theories to superior ones; instead, there are occasional jumps between alternatives, with no adequate way of judging which is better.[9] Paul Feyerabend went further: 'Knowledge ... is not a series of self-consistent theories that converges towards an ideal view; it is not a gradual approach to the truth. It is rather an ever-increasing *ocean of mutually incompatible (and perhaps even incommensurable) alternatives*, each single story, each fairy tale, each myth that is part of the collection forcing the others into greater articulation.'[10]

Conclusion

It is as though we have gone full circle. In the past many societies believed they could observe a bit of order carved out of a fundamental chaos, so they had a bit of knowledge but it could all change at any time. As long as people thought like this, science could not develop.

Science became possible when societies changed their views about the gods and developed a stronger conviction about order: that it is permanently built into the way things are by a God who has deliberately fixed it like that. This change first took place in western Europe. Over time the successes of science made it seem self-justifying, as though there was no need to invoke God as the cause of order.

Once God is taken out of scientific explanation, there is no longer any reason to presume that there is more order in the universe than science has so far established. The most we can say is that it happens to be regular for reasons we cannot fathom. However, even this turns out to be an exaggeration; it would be more accurate to say that the small fraction that we can observe happens to be regular – or better still, that this small fraction *seems to us* to be regular. We are back where we started, and for the same reason: in the cases of both ancient polytheism and postmodern non-realism, we have no reason to believe that there is more order than we have observed, or that the order we know will continue.

If this is the most we can say, most scientists would probably give up. Nearly all scientists believe there really is a real world outside their minds, that it is ordered, and that they are working out *how* it is ordered. If, as seems to be the case, they have no way of justifying these beliefs, then they are making an act of trust. They are committing themselves to presupposing things they cannot prove. What belief in God offers is a credible version of that act of trust, a reason for believing that our limited perceptions of order are by and large true, and that there is more order out there still to be discovered.

8

Intelligibility

———◆·◆·◆———

Over the course of this book it has become clear that a number of questions boil down to how much we trust the human mind. To most people, the world shows many signs of having been intentionally designed; but it is possible that our minds are deceiving us, and if we commit ourselves to the principle that nobody has designed it we can develop the art of not seeing any design in it. Similarly, values and morality play an important part in everybody's life: they seem to be real, objective features of the way things are, but it is possible to believe that our minds deceive us and they are really nothing but our own fictions. Again, the figures cited in Chapter 5 indicate that most people have at least one significant religious experience in their lives, but perhaps that too is a trick of the mind.

Where do we stop? You may think you are reading this book, but sometimes you get things wrong. How do you know your beliefs are *ever* true?

I am not a psychologist or a neurologist, but even if I were the world's greatest expert on the mind, all my expertise would depend on *presupposing* that the ideas in my own mind more or less represent the way things really are. Let us now explore where this leaves us. The main religious traditions teach that God has created the universe and has also designed our minds to understand it. Can an alternative theory without God work as well? As in the last chapter, I shall begin with some ancient theories that deny the reliability of human knowledge and move on to modern equivalents.

The most extreme denial we know of comes from certain Gnostic texts of the second century CE. Some Gnostic writings take an extremely negative view of the world and human life. A common story is that there was once just a single good god, either alone or in competition with an evil god. One thing led to another, things went wrong, and the evil or stupid god created the world. This god is often identified with the God of the Old Testament. An element of the good god then fell to earth. The evil gods controlling the earth wanted to keep that element there, and so created human bodies, putting a little bit of the good god into each body. As a result we are all created evil but we contain a spark of the good god. The ancient Greeks usually understood humans to be two things, body and soul – the soul being roughly the same as the mind. Gnostic myths often give us three elements: the body and soul created by the evil gods, but also this spark of the divine, the spirit. The point was to distinguish between the way most people normally think, which is complete error, and the truth buried deep within us which can be woken up.

Various myths describe how the supreme good god sends a messenger or redeemer from the realms above down to this earth to tell us about our real condition. This messenger is often Jesus. Jesus has to enter the evil world, a risky venture because it is governed by evil gods, so he takes the form of a human to deceive them. He warns people that the world is evil and tells them how after death their spirit can ascend back into heaven. When people accept the message, they learn to despise all physical life and long for the day when their spirit will be freed from its bodily prison. A poem by one Gnostic group, the Mandeans, runs:

> From the day when I came to love the Life, from the day when my heart came to love the Truth, I no longer have trust in anything in the world. In father and mother . . . In brothers and sisters I have no trust in the world . . . In what is made and created I have no trust in the world. In the whole world and its works I have no trust in the world. After my soul alone I go searching about, which to me is worth generations and worlds. I went and found my soul – what to me are all the worlds? . . . I went and found Truth as she stands at the outer rim of the worlds.[1]

Today the myths are different, but the basic idea that the normal human mind completely misunderstands reality is still popular in some Christian circles. These groups make a sharp distinction between their beliefs, which they consider directly revealed by God, and other people's beliefs, which they dismiss as the erroneous products of the mere human mind.

The idea suffers from a fundamental weakness. If the human mind is normally deceived about the nature of reality, how can they be sure the message they have received is not also erroneous? Because the question can always be asked, this kind of theory tends to generate countless sects competing against each other.

The second-century Catholics denounced the Gnostics as heretics and defended the Jewish principle that one good God created the world and designed human minds to understand it. This was so important to them that when the western Roman Empire collapsed, it was the Christian Church that became the main sponsor of scientific learning. It remained so for over a thousand years; this is why the debates over Copernicus and Galileo were so significant.

The principle did not get seriously examined again until the early Enlightenment, and even then it was only a question of fitting it into a new rational structure. Descartes began with himself, deduced the existence of God, and then argued: 'I recognize that it is impossible that he [God] should ever deceive me, since in all fraud and deceit is to be found a certain imperfection; and although it may seem that to be able to deceive is a mark of subtlety and power, yet the desire to deceive bears evidence without doubt of weakness or malice, and, accordingly, cannot be found in God.'[2]

In effect Descartes was continuing the Catholic tradition that God has designed our minds to understand the world. Empiricists agreed; Locke wrote: 'The infinite wise Contriver of us, and all things about us, hath fitted our senses, faculties, and organs, to the conveniences of life, and the business we have to do here. We are able, by our senses, to know and distinguish things.'[3]

Determinism

Slowly this consensus broke down. By the end of the eighteenth century two major changes had taken place in the understanding of knowledge. One was that reason was taken to be self-authenticating, so that there was no need to justify it. The human mind, it was thought, can work out scientifically how the universe functions, on the basis that everything that happens is caused by something else. The other was the rise of materialism. Instead of two realms, the physical one which we are learning about and the spiritual one where human minds think, the radical Enlightenment settled for just one realm, the physical universe operating entirely according to eternal laws of cause and effect. This meant that determinism applies to human minds: in other words, we have no real freedom of thought because all our thoughts are caused by something else, which was in turn caused by something else, all the way back to the Big Bang.

These two changes are widely accepted today. It is less often recognized that they contradict each other.

If our minds are determined, we have no 'open futures'. If your colleague offers you tea or coffee and you say you would like tea, determinists accept that you are free in the sense that you are choosing what you want. What it claims is that you did not have an open future: in exactly that situation you were bound to choose tea, even though you think you were free to choose coffee.

If determinism is true many normal human activities are completely misguided, chiefly blaming, thanking, deciding, and all moral judgements. They are misguided because none of us could have done other than we do. Some philosophers argue that believing in free will is misguided, yet is necessary for the good of society.[4]

Determinism undermines knowledge by denying an essential feature of knowing. If I toss a coin, claiming to know it will land up heads, and it does, my claim to have known is only true if I knew the coin had heads on both sides. If it was an ordinary coin I was just making a 50 per cent guess. To know something, we need to do more than just hold an opinion which happens to be true; the opinion must be *based on* the reasons why it is true. There needs to be a *free mental decision* that the reasons are sound.

Another example will illustrate the details. Judy believes that Paris is the capital of France. She read it in a book. If all our beliefs are determined, she would like to think that her belief about Paris is somehow caused by Paris actually being the capital of France. It may be indirect causation, but if her belief would have been caused whether or not Paris is the capital of France, she has no reason for supposing that her belief is true.

So how does Paris being the capital of France end up influencing the thoughts in Judy's mind? We can try it in two ways, following different theories about the mind. Some believe there is no such thing as the human mind over and above brain processes; so if we could wire Judy's brain up to a machine which describes the exact state of her brain, and give names to all her possible brain states, we may find that her belief in Paris being the capital of France is caused by her neurons being in state 12347. In that case, what caused her neurons to be in state 12347? Presumably the electrical currents from her eyes, which were in turn caused by the rays of light from the page of the book, which were in turn caused by the shapes of the ink on the page. We need to get all the way from Paris like this, with every effect physically caused, so that the end product in her brain accurately matches the reality hundreds of miles away. Hardly surprisingly, the people who think this is how it works tend to be non-realists, willing to treat the existence of Paris as just a linguistic convention. As the scientist J. B. S. Haldane said, 'If my mental processes are determined wholly by the motions of atoms in my brain, I have no reason to suppose that my beliefs are true. They may be sound chemically, but that does not make them sound logically. And hence I have no reason for supposing my brain to be composed of atoms.'[5]

Other determinists believe that although the mind depends on the brain, we have mental processes which cannot be explained in terms of physical processes (just as there are biological processes which cannot be explained by the laws of physics, even though they depend on the laws of physics). If so, it becomes easier to get to Judy's mind from Paris. She thinks Paris is the capital of France because she read it in a book which she trusts, and the book was written by somebody who knows about these things. This makes the sequence of causes more credible; but if determinism is true Judy still had no choice about holding her belief. If she now asks herself whether the book is reliable, or whether she rightly remembers reading it, determinism means that she will get no further forward: the fact that she asks these questions was just as determined, and whatever answer she comes up with will also be determined. Because *all* her thoughts are determined, she can never step outside her set of determined beliefs to judge which if any of them are true.

To make matters worse, if *everybody's* thoughts are determined, nobody can make a free, informed judgement about the relationship between Paris and France, or about anything else either.[6] In this way determinism about the human mind ends up refuting itself: if it is true, we have no way of knowing whether it is true.

Elitism

Many leading scientists have avoided facing up to this weakness in the determinist case by adopting a type of elitism. In effect they argue as though their minds are completely different from the minds of the people they are studying. I have already mentioned one example. Some determinist philosophers think belief in free will is erroneous but necessary for the good of society. What this means is: you and I know that there is no free will, nudge nudge wink wink, so all talk of morality, and all blaming and thanking, is completely misconceived: but other people need to believe in free will for the good of society. This is clearly too elitist to be credible: if it would be a social disaster for other people to find out the truth, why is it not a disaster for you and me to find it out? You and I should be prime suspects for undermining society.

Ever since the eighteenth century, when the high estimation of human reason was combined with materialism, the elitist tendency has been strong: 'we' the enlightened ones know best what is good for 'people'. 'They' do not know because their minds are determined. A well-known example is B. F. Skinner, a leading behaviourist. Skinner believed all human behaviour results from conditioning: when our actions get rewarded, we repeat them. The concept of the mind is a fiction and we have no real freedom. He expressed this clearly in his book *Beyond Freedom and Dignity* (1971). The book also expresses a strong concern to improve the lot of human life, a task which, Skinner tells us, should be performed by abandoning the false ideas of freedom and dignity and instituting a regime of positive and negative reinforcers to condition behaviour:

In what we may call the pre-scientific view . . . a person's behaviour is at least to some extent his own achievement. He is free to deliberate, decide, and act, possibly in original ways, and he is to be given credit for his successes and blamed for his failures. In the scientific view . . . a person's behaviour is determined by a genetic endowment traceable to the evolutionary history of the species and by the environmental circumstances to which as an individual he has been exposed . . . the second view shows a marked advantage when we begin to do something about behaviour . . . The environment can be changed, and we are learning how to change it.[7]

This passage illustrates elitism in two ways. First, at the beginning of it he denies that human beings are free to deliberate, decide and act on our decisions, but at the end he is confident that 'we' can. Second, it is central to behaviourist theory that our thoughts do not affect our behaviour. They are mere by-products of brain processes. This means that if the theory is true, the reason why he did his research is that he was being rewarded for it, regardless of whether it was true. Of course, the way he described the development of his theory was quite different. He did not describe it purely in terms of conditioning. He used mental language – about looking at the evidence and thinking about which were the best hypotheses. He often noted that people accused him of being inconsistent in these ways, but he could not produce a satisfactory response.

> It is central to behaviourist theory that our thoughts do not affect our behaviour

Skinner was one of many: the literature of determinists explaining how 'we' can improve the lot of determined humanity repeats this contradiction countless times. This does not make their theories useless. Each theory may well explain *some* human behaviour. It is when it is treated as an explanation of *all* human behaviour that it cannot escape applying to itself, and thereby refuting itself.

Science therefore depends on two different processes, one determined and the other undetermined. The information it gathers is about determined processes: whatever happens is the effect of causes, and those causes are in turn effects of other causes. If the sun was really free to decide for itself whether to rise tomorrow morning, science would be unable to predict whether it will. Determinism works on this level. However, if our minds were determined in the same way, we could never find out whether any of our thoughts are true.

Non-realists can be content with this conclusion, arguing that the world we are caused to believe in is the only world we can ever know about so we may as well treat it *as though* it was the real world. Most scientists,

> If the sun was really free to decide for itself whether to rise tomorrow morning, science would be unable to predict whether it will

on the other hand, think they are studying the real world, not just inventions of their minds. If they are right, they must accept that our minds are free, and therefore cannot be deterministically explained by science.

Thus our knowledge in general, including the sciences, depends on presuppositions we cannot prove. The key ones are:

- that there is a physical universe, which we can perceive through our eyes, ears and other senses;
- that the universe is ordered in a deterministic way, so that some future events can be predicted by suitable minds;
- that the human mind, despite being a product of the universe (via the brain) somehow bucks the deterministic trend and can freely think undetermined thoughts.

Many have found these hypotheses too difficult to reconcile with each other. I have tried to show that if we do not believe them all, we know nothing.

Once again it was David Hume who first noted the problem. Hume asked how we can know that our five senses perceive the world as it really is: indeed, how can we know there is a world outside our minds at all? To the inherited answer that a good God would not deceive, he replied that we have no proofs that there is a God at all, let alone one who would not deceive. His own way of coping with the uncertainty reveals commendable honesty: 'I dine, I play a game of backgammon, I converse, and am merry with my friends; and when after three or four hours' amusement, I wou'd return to these speculations, they appear so cold, and strain'd and ridiculous, that I cannot find in my heart to enter into them farther.'[8] In other words he admitted that he did not have an answer.

Today the usual approach is to offer an evolutionary answer: the ability to work out what is true should have given us an evolutionary advantage at some stage in our history. The way it would work is by adaptation and exaptation. Adaptation means those members of a species better suited to a particular environment have more surviving offspring, so the species gradually changes. Exaptation means a change caused by adaptation turns out to be useful for a different purpose than the original one.

I see no reason to doubt this account. Despite the claims of anti-evolutionists and militant atheists, there is nothing specifically atheistic about it; for the believer it is the best available account of *how* God gave free thought to humans. We do not need to presume an exact plan by God – maybe God would have been equally content if humans had died out and horses had developed the kinds of brains we have – but if God intended the existence of beings something like us, God would have designed the world to make it possible for those beings to exist.

To attribute the process to God does, however, make a difference. To posit an intending mind behind it is to presume that it has a purpose. The Gnostic account claims that the purpose is to mislead us while the early Catholic account claims that the purpose is to give us true information. The atheist account denies any purpose at all. The significance of this denial is often overlooked because atheistic eulogies of evolution often treat it as though it does have a purpose. They often treat humans as the product of progress, perhaps even the pinnacle of progress; but this, as we saw in Chapter 3, is to smuggle religious ideas into the picture.

> Atheistic eulogies of evolution often treat ... humans as the product of progress, perhaps even the pinnacle of progress

From an atheistic perspective it is possible to give an evolutionary account of how humans can access truth; the basic principle would be that the more often our beliefs about reality are true, the better our chances of survival are. However, it is equally possible to give an evolutionary account of how humans *cannot* access truth. Darwin had his concerns: 'The horrid doubt always arises whether the convictions of man's mind, which has been developed from the mind of the lower animals, are of any value or at all trustworthy. Would anyone trust in the convictions of a monkey's mind, if there are any convictions in such a mind?'[9]

When we compare evolution-as-a-God-given-process with evolution-as-a-result-of-impersonal-laws-of-nature, it becomes clear that evolution on its own does *not* show that our minds can access reality. All it shows is that *if* our minds access reality, evolution may explain the process. It still leaves open the possibility that evolution has only given our minds enough true information to help our Stone Age ancestors to survive; or even that evolutionary theory is itself an example of the human mind misunderstanding reality.

Most of us would like to believe that our minds do access reality. If we cannot justify this belief, perhaps the ancient Gnostics were right and our minds are completely deceived; or perhaps non-realists are right and we know nothing about any world which may or may not exist outside our minds.

One option is to assume we can understand reality, and abandon any attempt to justify the assumption. This is a pragmatist conclusion. Such pragmatism, as we have already seen, is unpopular among scientists because they see their task in terms of seeking explanations. If, on the other hand, we do set out to justify the assumption, our starting point will be that we cannot prove we know anything at all. What we must aim for is a hypothesis to explain how the presuppositions I listed can all be true, and can fit together consistently. If we can think of such a hypothesis, we can then test it by asking questions about it.

Such a hypothesis is contained in the theory that a benevolent divine mind has intentionally created the universe, and has designed human minds to understand it well enough for legitimate human purposes. There have been times in religious history – like the early Catholic reaction against the Gnostics – when this hypothesis has been an explicit claim.

Once again, it seems, science is not self-explanatory. In order to make sense of it, we have to believe there is more to reality than science can discover. We have to believe that this something more provides human minds with the power to think freely about the nature of reality. Either science works and religious belief works, or neither works.

Conclusion

This book has aimed to show that believing in God makes sense. The main focus has been to disagree with atheism, though I have also disagreed with the dogmatic religious traditions which are equally committed to denying that belief in God makes sense.

In Chapter 1 I described how these two traditions developed in close association with each other. Thereafter each chapter has focused on one of the main reasons for believing in God. In Chapter 2 we looked at the common impression that the world around us has been intentionally designed. None of the traditional arguments *proves* intentional design. This means not that the world is undesigned, but that it *could be* undesigned. If it is undesigned, though, science cannot account for it. We are used to imagining that the laws of nature can explain the world, but this is only because we often treat them as gods – in particular, attributing purposes and physical power to them. When we remember that the laws of nature are only observed regularities, lacking purpose or power, it becomes clear that science only notes regularities; it never establishes causal forces. To deny intentional design, therefore, is to deny that there is any explanation for the existence of the world or the way it works.

> We are used to imagining that the laws of nature can explain the world, but this is only because we often treat them as gods

It also empties the world of the values which give our lives significance, and this was the theme of Chapter 3. Atheism has no way to account for values as real features of our lives; either all our values are pure error or we create our own. Self-created values, however, can never do what we normally expect values to do. They can never reveal to us what is good and what is bad, what is worth doing and what is worth avoiding, because if they are our own creations they can only reveal to us what we have told them to reveal. Values only work as values when they relate our lives to something bigger than ourselves, something which makes our lives worthwhile. Ultimately, we can only make sense of our values if they relate to something bigger and more valuable than we can understand.

Chapter 4 continued the theme, with a focus on morality. Again, atheists have no way to account for moral truths except as human inventions. However, if there are no moral truths embedded in reality independently of the human mind, our self-created moral rules cannot do what we normally understand morality to do. They are unlikely to tell us that we ought not to do what we want to do, because we have programmed them to tell us what we want them to tell us. The only kind of morality which can have authority to pass judgement on what we want is a morality located in a mind more authoritative than our own minds.

Chapter 5 described personal religious experiences. Large numbers of people are convinced that they have been in the presence of some kind of greater being, and this has led them to change their lifestyles. Once again the evidence is not of the usual empirical type; the experience is not one of ordinary seeing or hearing, and it is possible to argue that it is just a quirk of the human mind, common though it is. People who have religious experiences, however, do consider them authentic, distinguish them quite sharply from the effects of drugs or epilepsy, and afterwards remember them as major life-changing events. Atheists reply that the experiences are unreliable because they do not come through the usual five senses. Thus they resort once again to positivist principles, denying the reality of experiences which cannot be empirically established, but this time emptying out the human mind rather than the physical world.

The following three chapters examined more theoretical issues. We think we know things – in fact we tend to think modern western society knows a lot more than other societies, because of the achievements of science. However, neither knowledge in general nor science in particular is self-explanatory. They depend on particular presuppositions. When we ask what those presuppositions are, it turns out that modern science only became possible in the context of some very specific convictions about God. Chapter 6 explored the case for a necessary being, through the ontological and cosmological arguments. Chapter 7 described how the world came to be seen as sufficiently ordered, by a particular kind of god, to make science seem credible. Chapter 8 described how the human mind came to be trusted as competent to understand the ways of nature. In each of these chapters I have tried to show that modern science depends on some claim about a divine being. Whereas atheists characteristically treat science and the existence of God as opposites, I have tried to show that if there is any truth in science, the existence of God must be true as well.

By now I hope to have shown that it does make sense to believe in God. Dogmatic religion characteristically asks people to accept too many unjustified beliefs; atheism, on the other hand, asks people to accept too little. It remains theoretically possible that atheism is correct. The possible options are of three types.

The first is the thoroughgoing nihilism proposed by Nietzsche and produced by consistent positivists. On this account reality consists of physical things doing what they do in accordance with regularities scientists have observed; all impressions of design, values, morality and divine beings are misleading tricks of the human mind. The way to explain each complex process is by reducing it to simpler processes. Everything that looks impressive is to be explained as 'nothing but' something simpler. This type of explanation, known as 'reductionism', is popular among those keen to show that reality can be explained by the human mind. In the case of the physical sciences there is no choice but to accept the new dimensions of reality; the atom, after all, has been split. In the case of the biological and social sciences there is still a strong tendency to reduce awe-inspiring complexities to 'nothing but' simple physical processes.

We can, if we try, go through life describing every pleasure, every excitement, every awe-inspiring discovery, as nothing but a simple, value-free physical process: every heroic endurance of torture and death is just people doing what they were brought up to do, every birth of a baby is just mothers doing what they have evolved to do. A few atheists try to explain all life in these terms. Rather more do so selectively. A person who believes we create our own moral codes, but regardless of theory jumps into a dangerous sea to rescue a drowning child, may explain the action in reductionist terms: 'There was nothing morally good about what I did; it's just the way I chose to behave.' People admire how the world is ordered to be just what it needs to be for life to flourish; but perhaps this is nothing but the product of unintending, impersonal laws of nature. We all find some things in our lives meaningful, valuable and purposeful, and we hope to make progress towards our purposes; but perhaps all these values are nothing but human inventions. We convince

> 'There was nothing morally good about what I did; it's just the way I chose to behave.'

ourselves and each other that some types of behaviour are morally right or wrong, but perhaps this too is nothing but a result of the way our kind of primate evolved. Many people have experiences which convince them of the presence of a divine reality, but perhaps once again this is nothing but a trick of the human mind.

All this could be true; but upon examination it is difficult to explain how. We cannot empty the universe of all meaning and complexity like this without also emptying ourselves. If we ourselves are nothing but chemical processes obeying undesigned impersonal laws of nature, we have no reason to suppose we can ever know anything at all. We cannot stand outside all human minds, observing from an objective standpoint how the human mind happens to produce beliefs about reality. If we try, we are talking about ourselves and must apply our theories to ourselves. If values, morals and spiritualities can be 'explained away' as nothing but the products of human evolution, then so can science – and so can whatever you are thinking right now.

In the way he reduced knowledge to sensory experience, Ernst Mach had a point. If the only things we really know are the bits of information we receive through the five senses, then perhaps all we can ever know is that we receive impressions of shapes, colours, sounds, feelings and smells. Moreover, if our minds are nothing but unintended products of the laws of nature, then all our theories about the nature of reality are nothing but products of the chemical processes in our brains. We – or rather you, as the rest of us may not exist – have no way of finding out whether your thoughts bear any resemblance to any world which may exist outside your mind. Thus we end up with an extreme non-realist position. In practice, even the most hardened positivist makes stronger claims for the powers of the human mind and the world's order.

The second type of option is what we might call popular atheism. It affirms that the world seems impressively ordered and that we can find peak experiences meaningful; but it affirms them only as human experiences, not as independent truths about reality. We feel positive about them only because we have evolved to feel positive about them. Similarly it affirms that life is full of meaning, value and moral standards, but it affirms them only as human creations, not as evidence of values which are there anyway. I hope to have shown that this position, popular though it is today, only seems credible because it borrows extensively from religious interpretations. The atheist who admires the order in the world is either performing some kind of worship, thus treating the laws of nature as gods, or is simply registering an error of the human brain, a tendency to admire that which is not really admirable. The borrowing is most obvious in the cases of values and morality. Characteristically, people who claim to have created their own values and moral standards feel as strongly as anyone else the real differences between good and bad, right and wrong. Whatever they claim in theory, they do not in practice treat their values as nothing but personal inventions. If they did, they would have to acknowledge that all their valuing and judging, all their thanking and resenting, all their praising and blaming, is just their own personal game of 'let's pretend'.

There are, of course, many versions of atheism, but all of them are caught in this tension. The more they deny, the less they can explain of the ordinary human experience of life; but the more they affirm, the more they are driven to betray their own principles, taking ideas which, they claim, are mere inventions of the human mind, and treating them like deep truths about reality.

I therefore believe the third type of option makes better sense. It means following Aquinas rather than Mach. Faced with the ordinary things of life, positivists advised reducing them to their simplest parts and excluding anything which cannot be perceived through the senses. Aquinas advised the opposite. When we reflect on what we think we know, we discover new dimensions of reality. This happens persistently – in the physical, biological and social sciences, let alone in spiritual matters. Reality keeps turning out to be far more complex than we previously thought. As we admire and study the things we

112

know about we keep discovering greater depths, unexpected entities, new dimensions of reality. We never get to a complete explanation of anything; wherever we look, we find complexities far beyond what we can understand.

The more we examine the world around us and our own relationship to it, the greater, more beautiful, more valuable, more admirable it turns out to be. This naturally fills us with a strange combination of feelings: awe at the complexity of reality and our own comparative smallness, but also awe at our mind's ability to engage with these complexities at all. Awe easily turns to veneration.

Although reality is always greater and more complex than we can understand, we can say some things about it: somewhere in that beyond-our-understanding there is benevolent creativity, and therefore mind, intention, wisdom, purpose, value, meaning and goodness. If we think this is what reality is like, it is natural to find it exciting – and respond with gratitude, praise and celebration.

Notes

Introduction

1 Perhaps best known are Richard Dawkins, *The Selfish Gene* (Oxford: OUP, 1976) and *The God Delusion* (London: Transworld, 2007). Also Christopher Hitchens, *God is Not Great* (London: Atlantic, 2007). Daniel Dennett's books are much more closely argued: see *Darwin's Dangerous Idea* (London: Penguin, 1995) and *Breaking the Spell: Religion as a Natural Phenomenon* (London: Penguin, 2006).

1 Our very strange situation

1 Mircea Eliade, *A History of Religious Ideas* (Chicago: University of Chicago Press, 1978), pp. 143–4.
2 There is a good discussion of this in M. M. Adams, *William Ockham* (Notre Dame: University of Notre Dame Press, 1987), pp. 966–7.
3 Observability has long been debated in the philosophy of science. There are discussions of the issue in Anthony O'Hear, *An Introduction to the Philosophy of Science* (Oxford: OUP, 1991) and Richard Boyd et al., *The Philosophy of Science* (Massachusetts: MIT Press, 1992).
4 The arguments are found in his *Discourse on Method* and *Meditations*.
5 John Locke, *An Essay Concerning Human Understanding* (London: Collins, 1984), 1.2. There is a discussion of these points in John Dunn et al., *The British Empiricists* (Oxford: OUP, 1992), Chapter 3.
6 Augustine, *City of God*, 21.8.
7 Locke, *Essay*, 4.15, 16.
8 David Hume, *Enquiries Concerning Human Understanding and Concerning the Principles of Morals* (Oxford: OUP, 11th impression 1990 of 3rd edn 1975), pp. 119–20.
9 Maurice Mandelbaum, *History, Man and Reason: A Study in Nineteenth Century Thought* (Baltimore: Johns Hopkins University Press, 1971), pp. 10–12.
10 Frederick C. Beiser, *The Sovereignty of Reason: The Defence of Rationality in the Early English Enlightenment* (Princeton: Princeton University Press, 1996), pp. 143–6.

11 A good account of the rationale behind fundamentalism is Harriet Harris, *Fundamentalism and Evangelicals* (Oxford: Clarendon, 1998).

12 For evangelical developments, see, D. W. Bebbington, *Evangelicalism in Modern Britain: A History from the 1730s to the 1980s* (Grand Rapids, MI: Baker, 1992). For the parallel change in Roman Catholicism, see Darrell Jodock, ed., *Catholicism Contending with Modernity: Roman Catholic Modernism and Anti-Modernism in Historical Context* (Cambridge: CUP, 2000).

13 Gerald O'Collins, 'Dogma', in Alan Richardson and John Bowden, eds, *A New Dictionary of Christian Theology* (London: SCM, 1989).

14 The classic text describing this view of doctrine is George Lindbeck, *The Nature of Doctrine: Religion and Theology in a Postliberal Age* (London: SPCK, 1984).

2 Design

1 R. Attfield, *Creation, Evolution and Meaning* (Aldershot: Ashgate, 2006), pp. 98–9.

2 There is a detailed analysis of Hume's critique of the design argument in J. C. A. Gaskin, *Hume's Philosophy of Religion* (London: Macmillan, 1978).

3 This tradition is discussed in Clarence J. Glacken, *Traces on the Rhodian Shore: Nature and Culture in Western Thought from Ancient Times to the End of the 18th Century* (Berkeley and Los Angeles: Univ. California Press, 1967). See especially p. 423.

4 Glacken, *Traces*, p. 423.

5 There is a good discussion of Paley's argument and his relation to other thinkers of the time in Tess Cosslett, *Science and Religion in the Nineteenth Century* (Cambridge: CUP, 1984). This text is discussed in pp. 25–30.

6 Cosslett, *Science*, p. 2.

7 Richard Dawkins, *The Blind Watchmaker* (London: Norton, 1996), p. 6.

8 Cosslett, *Science*, pp. 7–8.

9 Ian Markham, *Against Atheism: Why Dawkins, Hitchens, and Harris are Fundamentally Wrong* (Chichester: Wiley-Blackwell, 2010), p. 68.

10 Attfield, *Creation*, p. 105; John Hick, *An Interpretation of Religion: Human Responses to the Transcendent* (Basingstoke: Macmillan, 1989), p. 85.

11 Attfield, *Creation*, p. 106.

12 Hick, *Interpretation*, pp. 86–7.

13 Richard Dawkins, *The God Delusion* (London: Transworld, 2007), pp. 146, 178.

3 Values

1 Quoted in J. L. Mackie, *Ethics: Inventing Right and Wrong* (London: Penguin, 1977), p. 38.

2 J. B. Bury, *The Idea of Progress: An Inquiry Into Its Growth and Origin* (New York: Dover Publications, 1955); Robert Nisbet, *History of the Idea of Progress* (London: Heinemann, 1980).

3 Abraham Edel, *Aristotle and His Philosophy* (Chapel Hill: University of North Carolina Press, 1982), pp. 61–4.

4 Mackie, *Ethics*, pp. 38–9.

5 R. Attfield, *Creation, Evolution and Meaning* (Aldershot: Ashgate, 2006), p. 155.

6 Mackie, *Ethics*, p. 34.

7 Friedrich Nietzsche, *The Will to Power*, trans. W. Kaufmann and R. J. Hollingdale (New York: Random House, 1975), p. 327, quoted in John Cottingham, *On the Meaning of Life* (London and New York: Routledge, 2003), pp. 11–12.

8 Richard Rorty, *Consequences of Pragmatism* (Minneapolis: University of Minnesota Press, 1982), p. xlii, quoted in Cottingham, *Meaning*, p. 16.

9 Erik Wielenberg, *Value and Virtue in a Godless Universe* (Cambridge: CUP, 2005), p. 26.

10 Cottingham, *Meaning*, p. 31.

11 Bertrand Russell, *Mysticism and Logic* (London: Longmans, 1919), quoted in Ian S. Markham, *Truth and the Reality of God* (Edinburgh: T. & T. Clark, 1998), p. 18.

12 Daniel C. Dennett, *Darwin's Dangerous Idea* (London: Penguin, 1995). See especially pp. 204ff, 401ff.

13 Aquinas, *Summa Theologiae*, 1.88.a2. F. Copleston discusses it in *Aquinas* (London: Penguin, 1988), pp. 59–60.

14 Cottingham, *Meaning*, pp. 78–9.

4 Morality

1 Alasdair MacIntyre, *After Virtue: A Study in Moral Theory* (London: Duckworth, 1985), p. 111.

2 MacIntyre, *After Virtue*, pp. 52–61.

3 American Declaration of Independence, 1776. <http://www.ushistory.org/declaration/document/>

4 French Revolution's 'Declaration of the Rights of Man and of the Citizen', 1789.

5 <http://www.un.org/en/documents/udhr/index.shtml>

6 S. Körner, *Kant* (London: Penguin, 1990), pp. 142–7.

7 Körner, *Kant*, p. 134.

8 MacIntyre, *After Virtue*, pp. 39–45.

9 Jeremy Bentham, *The Principles of Morals and Legislation* (1789), ch. I, p. 1.

10 Bentham, *Principles*, ch. IV.

11 J. L. Mackie, *Ethics: Inventing Right and Wrong* (London: Penguin, 1977), p. 35. Cf. pp. 48–9.

12 D. H. Monro, ed., *A Guide to the British Moralists* (London: Fontana, 1972), p. 14.

13 Erik Wielenberg, *Value and Virtue in a Godless Universe* (Cambridge: CUP, 2005), pp. 41–2.

14 W. D. Hudson, *Modern Moral Philosophy* (Basingstoke: Macmillan, 2nd edn 1983), pp. 314–33.

15 Hudson, *Modern Moral Philosophy*, pp. 107–11.

16 Charles Stevenson, *Ethics and Language* (New Haven: Yale University Press, 1944), pp. 21–6.

17 Quoted in Hans Küng, *Does God Exist?* (Oxford: OUP, 1978), p. 389.

18 Hastings Rashdall so argued in *The Theory of Good and Evil, Volume 2: A Treatise on Moral Philosophy* (Oxford: Clarendon, 1907), pp. 206–8.

5 Religious experience

1 Paul Badham, 'The Experiential Grounds for Believing in God and a Future Life', *Modern Believing*, vol. 46 no. 1 (January 2005), p. 34.

2 Marianne Rankin, *Religious and Spiritual Experience* (London: Continuum, 2008), p. 4.

3 Rankin, *Experience*, pp. 13–14.

4 Rankin, *Experience*, pp. 91–2.

5 John Hick, *The New Frontier of Religion and Science: Religious Experience, Neuroscience and the Transcendent* (Basingstoke: Macmillan, 2006), p. 29.

6 Rankin, *Experience*, p. 3.

7 Badham, 'Experiential', p. 34.

8 Badham, 'Experiential', p. 34.

9 Rankin, *Experience*, pp. 234–8.

10 Hick, *New Frontier*, pp. 39–51.

11 Hick, *New Frontier*, p. 29.

12 Rankin, *Experience*, p. 5.

13 David Hay found that it is reported by 65 per cent of postgraduates, 56 per cent of those educated beyond the age of 20 but only 29 per cent of those who left school at 15; 49 per cent of people in professions,

32 per cent of unskilled workers. Paul Badham, *The Contemporary Challenge of Modernist Theology* (Cardiff: University of Wales Press, 1998), p. 131.

14 Hick, *New Frontier*, pp. 68–9.

15 Rankin, *Experience*, p. 2.

16 Rankin, *Experience*, p. 140.

17 Rankin, *Experience*, p. 5.

18 Rankin, *Experience*, p. 5.

19 Rankin, *Experience*, p. 5.

20 Rankin, *Experience*, p. 93.

21 Hick, *New Frontier*, p. 74.

22 Hick, *New Frontier*, p. 130.

23 Hick, *New Frontier*, p. 131.

24 Hick, *New Frontier*, p. 137.

25 Hick, *New Frontier*, p. 149.

26 Badham, 'Experiential', p. 35.

27 Hick, *New Frontier*, pp. 145, 164.

28 Hick, *New Frontier*, p. 138.

29 Hick, *New Frontier*, pp. 140–2.

30 Rankin, *Experience*, p. 239.

31 Badham, 'Experiential', p. 38.

32 Rankin, *Experience*, p. 155. The figure of 82 per cent is on p. 156.

33 Rankin, *Experience*, p. 162.

34 Rankin, *Experience*, p. 163.

35 Badham, 'Experiential', p. 38.

36 Badham, 'Experiential', p. 38.

37 Rankin, *Experience*, pp. 164, 246.

38 Rankin, *Experience*, p. 162.

39 Badham, 'Experiential', p. 37.

40 Rankin, *Experience*, pp. 163–4; Badham, 'Experiential', p. 38.

6 Necessary being

1 John Hick, *The Existence of God* (London: Macmillan, 1964), p. 23.

2 Psalms 14.1; 53.1.

3 Geddes MacGregor, *Introduction to Religious Philosophy* (London: Macmillan, 1968), pp. 103–5.

4 See for example J. Hick and A. C. McGill, eds, *The Many-Faced Argument* (New York and London: Macmillan, 1976).

5 John Hick, *An Interpretation of Religion: Human Responses to the Transcendent* (Basingstoke: Macmillan, 1989), p. 76.

6 Hick, *Interpretation*, pp. 76–7.

7   Keith Ward, *Rational Theology And the Creativity of God* (Oxford: Blackwell, 1982), pp. 29–30.

8   Plato, *Laws*; Hick, *Existence*, pp. 71–9.

9   Hick, *Existence*, p. 80.

10 Aquinas, *Summa Theologiae* 1a, q. 2a.

11 Hick, *Existence*, p. 89; Ward, *Rational Theology*, p. 14.

12 Ward, *Rational Theology*, p. 14.

7 Order

1   Goldacre has a regular column 'Bad Science' in *The Guardian*.

2   Homer, *Iliad*, Book 21, trans. E. V. Rieu (Harmondsworth: Penguin, 1950), pp. 385–6.

3   Helmer Ringgren, *Religions of the Ancient Near East* (London: SPCK, 1973), p. 96.

4   Keith Thomas, *Religion and the Decline of Magic: Studies in Popular Beliefs in Sixteenth- and Seventeenth-Century England* (London: Penguin, 1971), pp. 689–90.

5   Christopher Kaiser, *Creation and the History of Science* (London: Marshall Pickering, 1991), p. 154.

6   Kaiser, *Creation*, pp. 159–61.

7   David Hume, *Enquiries Concerning Human Understanding and Concerning the Principles of Morals* (Oxford: OUP, 11th impression 1990 of 3rd edn 1975), 7.2.60.

8   David Hume, *A Treatise of Human Nature*, ed. L. A. Selby-Bigge, 2nd edn revised by P. H. I. Nidditch (Oxford: OUP, 1978, 1989), quoted in John Dunn, J. O. Urmson and A. J. Ayer, *The British Empiricists: Locke, Berkeley, Hume* (Oxford: OUP, 1992), p. 251.

9   Richard Boyd et al., *The Philosophy of Science* (Massachusetts: MIT Press, 1992), pp. 12–13, 139–57.

10 Paul Feyerabend, *Against Method* (London, 1975), p. 30, quoted in R. Trigg, *Reality at Risk* (Brighton: Harvester, 1980), p. 62. The emphasis is Trigg's.

8 Intelligibility

1   Hans Jonas, *The Gnostic Religion* (London: Routledge, 1992), pp. 90–1. The Mandeans are the only Gnostic Christian church to survive today – in Iraq, where they have recently suffered intense persecution.

2   Descartes, René, *Discourse on Method and the Meditations*, London: Penguin, 1968, pp. 132–3.

3   John Locke, *An Essay Concerning Human Understanding* (London: Collins, 1984), 2.23.12.

4 George Graham, *Philosophy of Mind: An Introduction* (Oxford: Blackwell, 1993), p. 159, cites John Searle and Thomas Nagel as examples.
5 J. B. S. Haldane, *Possible Worlds and Other Essays* (London: Chatto & Windus, 1927), vol. 2, p. 470, quoted in Stanley L. Jaki, *The Purpose of It All* (Edinburgh: Scottish Academic Press, 1990), p. 153.
6 R. Trigg, *Reality at Risk* (Brighton: Harvester, 1980), pp. 148–9.
7 B. F. Skinner, *Beyond Freedom and Dignity* (Harmondsworth: Penguin, 1973 edition), p. 101.
8 J. C. A. Gaskin, *Hume's Philosophy of Religion* (London: Macmillan, 1978), p. 112.
9 Charles Darwin, Letter to Graham William, 3 July 1881, quoted in Paul Helm, ed., *Faith and Reason* (Oxford: OUP, 1999).

Printed in the USA
CPSIA information can be obtained
at www.ICGtesting.com
CBHW060725090624
9685CB00015B/136